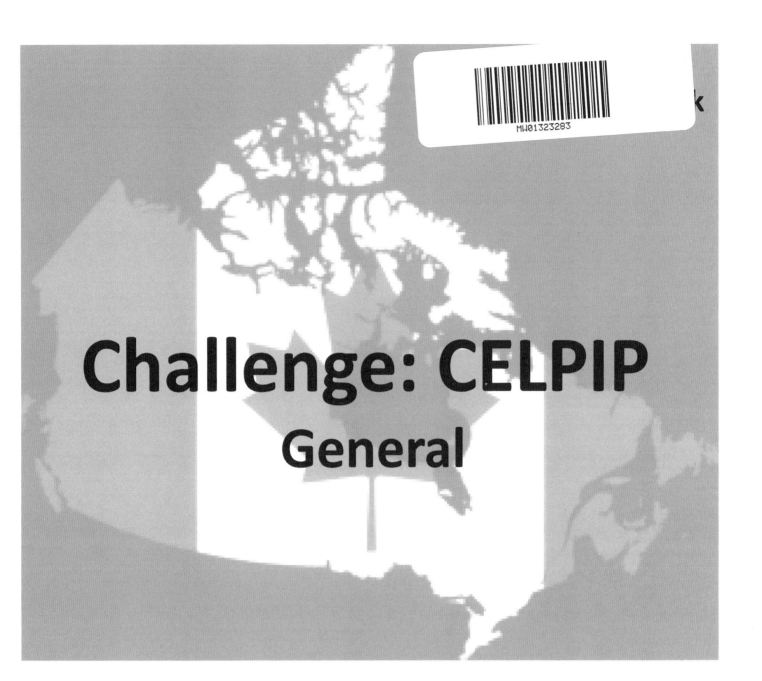

Challenge: CELPIP
General

Complete preparation course
for the CELPIP General exam

A. Christina Burnside

- In loving memory, this book is dedicated to Donald Taylor in answer to his question -

This CELPIP preparation course has been designed to help you achieve high marks on your exam. Every effort has been made to ensure sufficient practice for all areas of the exam.

The CELPIP exam is a computer based exam that focuses on the main areas of English as it relates to real-life situations in a Canadian setting. The vocabulary, idioms, tone and pronunciation are based on Canadian English and language use. While the knowledge and language skills you will gain from this course can be used in any English speaking country, it has been prepared to maximize your transition into life as a Canadian.

The content is based on Canada and to that end, you will not only gain valuable insight into the Canadian experience but this exam preparation course will assist you in understanding what it means to be Canadian.

The CELPIP is divided into 4 areas of testing. Your listening, reading, writing and speaking will be evaluated in different contexts and based on different topics. We have tried to cover a variety of topics that could appear on the exam so you not only have the vocabulary to succeed on the exam, but also to participate in conversations in these situations as well.

In the listening exam, you will be tested on your ability to comprehend in context, a variety of topics and select an appropriate response or identify a visual summary of what has been said. The listening exam gets progressively harder as you move through the sections. This will give you and the examiners a better idea of your skill level.

The reading exam requires a strong vocabulary and grammar base. You will be required to answer multiple choice questions as well as more grammar based exercises. Your attention to detail is crucial in this section and requires the ability to differentiate between parts of speech (nouns, verbs, etc.) and time (past, present, future). In order to succeed in this section, you need to build your vocabulary and your understanding of grammatical concepts.

The writing exam is often the part of the exam that students dislike the most. It can be the most difficult because strong punctuation and spelling skills are required in order to succeed. Writing an informal letter of 100-125 words and a formal letter of 150-170 words is required. It is important to ensure you have used proper planning, development, structure, style, punctuation and spelling.

The speaking test examines your ability to respond to various cues within a conversation and provide a summary of a situation. Speaking is the most utilized language skill as we communicate verbally every day and having a strong ability to contribute to and participate in conversations is very important.

We hope that after completing this course, you will have a better understanding of Canadian culture, values, traditions and language uses that will enable you to not only pass the CELPIP exam but that you will refer to this book in the future to help you maintain and grow your English language skills.

This course book is organized into 10 units, with each unit focusing on a different Canadian city. Within each unit is a brief grammatical overview and a collection of tasks that closely resemble those on the CELPIP exam.

We wish you the best of luck on the exam and hope you enjoy Canada as much as we do!

Legend of icons used in this book:

Content Guide to Challenge: CELPIP General

Topic	Skill	Test Area
1. Where am I? *Calgary*	Interrogative Pronouns Present simple, present continuous Prepositions of place Directions	Speaking: 1 Listening: 1, 5 Reading: 4
2. What did you say? *Toronto*	Past simple, past continuous Activity collocations Listening for key words Pronunciation – assessing tone	Reading: 3, 4 Listening: 5 Writing: 1 Speaking: 3
3. Who are you? *Regina*	Subject/Object Adjectives & Pronouns Future Noun/Verb Agreement Pronunciation – rising/falling intonation	Speaking: 2 Listening: 4, 5 Writing: 1 Reading: 3, 4
4. When is dinner? Grise Fiord	Countable/uncountable nouns Articles Sequencing words Food vocabulary	Reading: 2, 4 Speaking: 3
5. How long have you been here? Ottawa	Perfect tenses Conditionals	Reading: 1, 4 Speaking: 4
6. Why is it so warm? Vancouver	Comparatives/superlatives Environment vocabulary Technology vocabulary	Listening: 3
7. How much is that? Winnipeg	Conjunctions Money collocations Types of transportation	Reading: 3, 4 Speaking: 2, 3
8. How often do you go to the cinema? Montreal	Passives Art vocabulary Pronunciation – endings	Reading: 3, 4 Listening: 4 Speaking: 2
9. What do you do? Halifax	Work collocations Professions vocabulary	Reading: 2, 3 Listening: 5 Writing: 2
10. Are you ready? Canada	Talking about Canada Reading about Canada Writing about Canada Listening to Canadian Anthem	
Appendix	Prepositions Prefixes & Suffixes Synonyms, antonyms & homonyms Word family charts Irregular verb cue cards	Phrasal verbs Modal verbs Grammar practice Adjective chart

Where am I?

Grammar: Interrogative pronouns and present tenses

A

1. **Interrogative Pronouns**: These are words we use to start questions. Match the interrogative pronoun with the information it is asking. Use the interrogative pronouns in the box.

   _____ when you want to know the height
   _____ when you want to know the duration
   _____ when you want to know the person
   _____ when you want to know the age
   _____ when you want to know the reason
   _____ when you want to know the place
   _____ when you want to know the time
   _____ when you want to know the distance
   _____ when you want to know the number
   _____ when you want to know the quantity
   _____ when you want to know the frequency
   _____ when you want to know the thing
   _____ when you want to know the method, condition

Who	Where	How far	How often	When	How much
How	Why	How old	How many	What	How high
How long					

   ⭐ We use interrogative pronouns when we need information. Knowing these will help you not only with various parts of the exam, but in your day to day conversations. After practicing these, you will notice your level of comprehension increase, so be sure to study these often. They will be used throughout this book.

2. Complete the following sentences with the correct interrogative pronoun.

   1. _____ are you from? I'm from Brazil.
   2. _____ is your brother? He's 19.
   3. _____ is our class? It's 2 hours, from 9-11.
   4. _____ do you call your family? I call them every day.
   5. _____ away do you live from school? I live 4 km from school.
   6. _____ children do you have? I have 3 children. One son and two daughters.
   7. _____ is that man over there? I don't know. Maybe he is a new student.
   8. _____ water do you drink? I drink 4 glasses a day.
   9. _____ is your name? My name is Samantha.
   10. _____ do you spell your name? S-a-m-a-n-t-h-a
   11. _____ do you want to live in Canada? Because there are more jobs here.
   12. _____ is your office building? I think it is about 15 stories.
   13. _____ does it get cold in Canada? It gets cold in October.
   14. _____ do you want to go on vacation? Hawaii.
   15. _____ students in your class? There are 6.

3. Introduce yourself to the person beside you. Then ask questions like the ones above and think of your own questions too. Try to use as many interrogative pronouns as you can. Put the information into the box below. You will need to use it later.

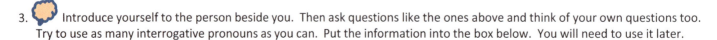

Application of Interrogative pronouns

4. 🔊 You are going to hear a conversation between two people in an airport. Listen to the conversation very carefully and answer the following questions. You should pay attention to interrogative pronouns as they will help you with the answers. You will only hear the conversation once. This is similar to Part 5 of the Listening exam.

1. Where does the person want to go?
2. How much does a taxi cost?
3. Why doesn't the person want to take a taxi?
4. How much is the shuttle bus?
5. How long is the trip?
6. Where is the person staying?
7. How often do the shuttle buses run?
8. When is the next shuttle bus?
9. How many tickets does the person want?
10. Where should the person wait?
11. Where is the person visiting for the first time?

⭐ Many people have better listening comprehension than reading after living in an English speaking country. Using audio books with questions is an excellent way to practice your comprehension skills. This can help you to recognize the spelling and pronunciation of words.

B

Present Simple: Be and other verbs

First, let's look at the verb *to be*. There are 3 forms in the present:
 a) am – we only use this with *I* – I **am** a teacher
 b) is – we only use this with *he, she, it* – She **is** my friend
 c) are – we only use this with *you, we, they* – They **are** students

The present simple is used to talk about the present time. There are some main ideas to remember:
 a) we use the present simple for **facts** – Water **boils** at 100°C
 b) we use the present simple for **routines** – I **walk** to work every day
 c) we use the present simple for **habits** – They **drink** coffee

Let's look at example a). Why did we add 's' to boil?_____
Let's look at example b). Why did we not add 's' to walk? _____
Let's look at example c). Why did we not add 's' to drink? _____

Spelling changes: When a verb ends in **ch**, **sh**, **ss** or **x**, we have to add "es" for he/she/it (match**es**, wash**es**, pass**es**)
 When a verb ends in **consonant + y**, we change the **y** to **i** and then add **es** (part**ies**, carr**ies**)

Making negatives: To make a sentence negative, insert the word *not* after the verb be and before other verbs: I am **not** hungry. She does not like to dance. They are not from Calgary. You do not speak Ukranian. Notice the use of the auxiliary verb.

Create the rule now:

When using the present simple, we add ____ or _____ to the main verb when the subject is _____, _____ or _____
When using the present simple, we do not add 's' to the main verb when the subject is _____, _____, _____, or _____

1. Complete the following sentences using the correct form of the verb given. Look at the rules above to help you.

1. Sally _____(walk) to school everyday.
2. My brother and I _____(like) swimming and golfing.
3. I_____(not play) the guitar and piano.
4. My cousin _____ (fix) cars.
5. Jane and Mary _____(live) in Calgary.
6. Kevin _____(not party) every weekend
7. The children _____(enjoy) arts and crafts.
8. She_____(not be) very good at photography.
9. They_____(be) very happy it is spring.
10. Canadians_____(love) hockey and baseball.
11. That guy_____(watch) too much tv!
12. Her brother_____(fly) a plane twice a month.

Being able to identify correct parts of speech is tested on the reading exam and is needed for the writing and speaking exams. Making subject /verb disagreement errors is a common mistake. Your ability to put sentences together correctly and identify disagreement is very important. It can be confusing to your listeners or readers if you make these mistakes and can cause misunderstandings.

To avoid these errors, practicing the grammar is important. Grammar books are useful but be careful not to overwhelm yourself by trying to complete a grammar book cover to cover. Focus on the grammar point specific to the exercise and practice it until it becomes automatic.

There is no such thing as too much practice so be sure to concentrate on this skill in your every day conversations

If you prefer using the internet and newspapers or media sources for practice, make sure you have a purpose. Simply watching tv, listening to the radio or reading a newspaper will not improve your skills without having a defined purpose. Here are some examples of defined purposes for using these resources:

a) Identify subject and/or verb and change them. If they are singular, make them plural and vice versa.
b) Create information questions for yourself. This will not only help your comprehension but your ability to identify information.
c) Write down 2 or 3 sentences that you hear that may be new for you and practice them. Remember the context in which you heard them.

Application of present tenses

2. Using the information you heard from your partner in Part A, exercise 3, write sentences in the present simple, following the rules we just learned. Make sure you use the correct verb form. For example: *Anja is from Poland. She is married and has 2 children.*

_____
_____
_____
_____
_____
_____
_____
_____
_____
_____
_____
_____
_____
_____

In Part 1 of the listening exam, you will have to identify the location of objects in relation to each other. This is also a valuable skill to have when explaining space and location relationships between objects and people. Practicing prepositions is sometimes challenging as they don't make sense in your language.

Practicing prepositions daily can be part of your commute to work. If you take the bus or train, select 2 objects and describe their location relationship. For example:

The woman in the red hat is *beside* the man in the blue coat and *in front of* the girl with the umbrella.

Part 2 of the speaking exam requires you to answer questions based on a map or diagram. Being able to give and receive directions as well as explaining and understanding locations is a part of every day life. Lets practice that now.

Grammar: Prepositions of place

C

In the recording in Part A, Exercise 4, there were several prepositions. These are very important to know and to understand for time, location and direction. Please remember to study these in English and not translate as sometimes they will not make sense in your language and you will get very confused. Use these boxes to help you. Where are the red ✖ ? For example, the ✖ is behind the box.

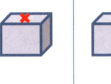   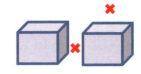

1. It often helps in the learning process to produce visual cues of what you are trying to learn. If you can create a visual representation correctly, you know you are well on your way to full comprehension. On a separate piece paper, draw basic pictures to represent the following sentences. 1-8.

2. 🔊 Now listen to the recorded sentences and draw the pictures.

    1. The woman is beside the stop sign
    2. The small dog is under the table
    3. The yellow fish is on the left of the rock
    4. The oranges are between the apples and bananas
    5. The short man is at the back of the line
    6. The children are in the pool
    7. The entrance is to the right of the window
    8. The woman is walking through the park

3. Look around the room. Using a dictionary if necessary, create ten sentences about the objects you see and where they are. Try to use as many prepositions as you can and make sure you are using the correct form of the verb.

Application of prepositions of place

4. Following the directions below, label the diagram below (1-10) with the things in the neighbourhood.

The school is labeled number (1).

Walk across the street. You are going to meet your friends for lunch at the bar 3 doors from the corner. Label that number (2). After lunch, you are going to move your things from your hotel (3) which is 3 blocks south and 3 blocks west of the bar. Then, you are going to go to your new accommodations at the B & B (4) which is due west of the hotel. Once you are settled, go to the grocery store and get some food. You have 2 choices; one is three blocks north on the right side of the street (5) and the other is three blocks east and two blocks north from the B &B (6). One is American and the other is Canadian. The Canadian store is closer to your accommodations. The bank you chose (7) and the University of Calgary downtown campus (8) are on the same avenue, three streets apart, with the campus being further west There is a great gift shop (9) just down the street from the American grocery store. You can buy some beautiful presents for your teacher there! Now that you know your neighbourhood, walk around to find an apartment to live in. There is a property management company (10) that looks after many buildings downtown and they are not far. You can find them on 8th Avenue between 9th and 10th Street.

Now, place 5 more locations on your map, anywhere. You are going to explain to your partner where you want them to go. These words and expressions will help you. Use the space below to make notes.

on the corner	across the street	kitty corner	up the street	down the street
	around the corner	on the right	on the left	

Introduction to Reading exam: Practice finding specific information

Read the article below and answer the following questions

A Magical City

Calgary is a thriving city of over 1 million people. It is located in the southern part of the province. While it is not the capital, it is currently the largest city in Alberta.

While there are some disagreements over how Calgary got it's name, some say it comes from The Norse words *kalt* and *gart*, meaning 'cold garden'. Others believe the name might come from the Gaelic language, *Cala ghearraidh*, meaning 'beach of the meadow '

It's location at the foot of the majestic Rocky Mountains and it's high elevation, make Calgary's climate variable. In the winter, it can be very cold. Calgarians are thankful, however, for Chinook winds that come over the mountains. These warming winds can increase winter temperatures as much as 20 degrees Celsius.

There is a strong senses of pride among Calgarians for several reasons. Primarily, Calgary was the first Canadian city to host the Winter Olympic Games, back in 1988. It was a tremendous success, incorporating many of the cultural and economic aspects of both the city and the region.

Secondly, during the summer months, not a weekend goes by without something to do. There is a plethora of cultural events in and around the city. From music and arts festivals to cultural and heritage events, there is something for everyone. Just one example of what is available is the Sun and Salsa Festival which takes place in Kensington. This event is great fort the whole family with music, vendors and, as the name suggests, a salsa judging contest.

There is a grand schedule of events planned for Canada Day on Prince's Island Park and in other areas throughout the city as well. And, of course, it is not possible to talk about Calgary events and culture without talking about the world famous Calgary Stampede.

The Calgary Stampede lasts for 10 magnificent days during July, and is kicked off on a Friday with a fantastic parade. Stampede Queens and Princesses, local businesses, various First Nations groups in traditional dress as well as military, emergency services and a large variety of people and animals all take part in this exceptional parade. The leader of the parade, the Marshall, is usually someone famous or noteworthy. For the 100th year celebration Prince William and Kate were honoured with the role of marshalling the parade. For Stampede 101, Col. Cmdr. Chris Hadfield, upon return from space, was the marshal.

The Stampede attracts people from all over the world. Cowboys, politicians, vendors and visitors flock to Calgary to experience the excitement.

> This kind of exercise will help you learn to identify main ideas and locate specific information. Being able to clearly identify information will help you with the multiple choice questions in Part 4 of the Reading exam.

1. How many people are there in Calgary?

2. Where is it located?

3. How much can Chinook winds increase winter temperatures?

4. Why are Calgarians proud?

5. Where does the Sun & Salsa festival take place?

6. What happens in July?

7. How long does the Stampede last?

8. Who marshalled Stampede 101?

9. Who comes to the Stampede?

Grammar: Making and answering questions

E

So how do we make questions? What is the construction? We learned earlier that interrogative pronouns are important for information, so they are first. Let's look at this construction.

Interrogative pronoun + auxiliary verb + subject + main verb

An auxiliary verb is just for grammar, it has no meaning, but don't forget it! Look at this example: **Where do you live?** This sentence follows our rule. If you don't want information, just a yes or no answer, drop the interrogative pronoun and add an activity or a noun.

Do you like dancing? Do they drive a car? Does she live in a house?

Because *like* and *drive* and *live* are action verbs, we use *do* to make our questions. If we have a question about a feeling or a want, we use the auxiliary verb *be*. Let's look at some examples.

Are you hungry? Are you ok?

In these examples, we are asking about a person's state or emotion so we use *be*. In these examples, we are still following our rule, but instead of nouns and activities, we finish our question with an adjective.

<u>Answering yes/no questions</u>

Positive answers: Yes, I am   Yes, she does   Yes, they have
Negative answers: No, I'm not   No, she doesn't   No, we haven't

We cannot use contractions in positive short answers. For example, we must use full form: Yes, I am.

The easiest way to remember is to listen to the auxiliary verb used in the question and repeat it. *Does she cook? Yes, she does.*

Application of making and answering questions

1. When we have a conversation, we usually ask lots of questions. We have now learned how to make information questions and yes/no questions. Using the sentences you created from the information you learned from your partner in Part B, exercise 2, write follow-up questions. For example: *How old are Anja's children?*

_____
_____
_____
_____
_____
_____
_____
_____
_____
_____

2. Looking at the article we read, Part D, make yes/no questions. For example, we read that *Calgary is currently the largest city in Alberta*. We can change this into a question: **Is Calgary Alberta's largest city?** Make 5 questions to ask your partner.

_____
_____
_____
_____
_____
_____

Grammar: Present continuous and comparison to present simple

F

The construction of the present continuous is _____ plus _____. An example is *I am sitting on a chair*

What is the difference in use between the present simple and the present continuous?

We use the present simple for _____
We use the present continuous for _____

To create present continuous questions, we _____

Let's examine: You are studying   Are you studying?   You are not studying
                 The sun is shining   Is the sun shining?   The sun isn't shining

Watch your spelling when changing a verb from the infinitive to the –ing form.

1. Complete the following sentences and questions using the present continuous.

    1. Where _____ you _____ (go) for Christmas? I _____ (not/go) anywhere.
    2. I _____ (practice) my verbs tonight.
    3. _____ they _____ (play) any sports this winter?
    4. Why _____ he _____ (look) at me like that?
    5. I _____(start) to feel sick so I _____(not go) to work today.
    6. They_____(try) to find a new home but they_____(not have) much luck.
    7. What _____ you_____(plan) to make for dinner?
    8. How long_____ she_____(stay) with you?
    9. I _____(not eat) that, it _____(still move)!
    10. Why _____ you_____(cry)? _____ you_____(feel) sad?
    11. We_____(come) to the party because it is too far for us.
    12. Thanks, but you_____(not help) the situation, please be quiet.

Application of present continuous and comparison to present simple

2. 🔊 Listen to the following conversation. You will hear a combination of present simple and present continuous. Write down as many examples of the present continuous as you can so we can compare them after the recording. For example, why did the man say *I'm calling* and not *I call*?

Using the correct tense during the writing exam is very important. It tells your reader about the time and the actions you are writing about. There is a big difference between *I drive* and *I am driving*. One is a statement of fact and refers to a general truth. The other suggests you are doing this action now, which, if you are writing an exam, isn't possible!	Please be aware of spelling changes when changing verbs into the continuous form. Common mistakes include
	  * not doubling final consonant (siting ✗, not sitting ✓)
	  * not dropping final 'e' before adding –ing ending (makeing ✗, not making ✓)
	  * changing state verbs into action verbs when you can't (we can't say *I am liking Canada*)

Your ability to write effectively will greatly improve your speaking skill. The more you write, the better you speak. All skills can be connected this way and are interdependent.

Review

Vocabulary to remember

Use this box to write any new vocabulary you learned in the unit

Write a short composition about Calgary using everything you have learned in the unit, adding more information if you can. For example, include the shuttle bus information you heard about, the location of some places, etc. Think about prepositions of place, present simple, present continuous. Use positive and negative forms. Do not include questions.

Using your composition above, create comprehension questions using both interrogative questions and yes/no questions

What did you say?

Grammar: Past simple

A

There are regular and irregular verbs. Regular past tense verbs end in –ed. Irregular past tense verbs have different forms.

Let's look at these examples: **Be**: am/is/are → was/were/been
Do: do/does → did/done

There are some change groups to help you remember more easily. They are

i/a/u → sing/sang/sung, ring/rang/rung
ught → teach/taught/taught, fight/fought/fought
same form → cut/cut/cut, let/let/let
en past participle → fall/fell/fallen, break/broke/broken
same past simple and past participle → have/had/had, light/lit/lit

Just like with the present tenses from unit 1, when we make questions or negatives, we follow the same rules. Here are examples to help you:

Did you **go** to the party last night? No, I **didn't go** to the party last night

Remember: For questions and negatives, we change the auxiliary verb but keep our main verb in infinitive form.

> Studying the past participle of irregular verbs is very important! Study study study! Select 5-10 irregular verbs to practice every day.
>
> The past participle of the verb is used in the passive, present perfect and past perfect tenses. Knowing and using these grammatical structures will help you understand more during the listening and reading exams as they identify the focus of a sentence, the sequence of events and time-action relationships.

Application of past simple

1. Complete these sentences with the correct form of the verb in the past.

   1. My brother Travis _____ (go) to Mexico last year for a holiday.
   2. _____ you and your friends_____ (have) lunch together last week?
   3. Where _____ you _____ (go) for dinner yesterday?
   4. She _____ (not/know) about the party because her friend _____ (forget) to tell her.
   5. When _____ they _____ (raise) the prices?
   6. They_____(know) about the dangerous conditions, but they _____(go) skiing anyway.
   7. How long _____he_____(stay) at the party? _____ he_____(become) drunk?
   8. Why _____you_____(not tell) me you_____(be) in town?
   9. I _____(study) for the exam but I _____(not realize) it_____(be) yesterday!
   10. My uncle _____(be) on vacation in Italy when the snowstorm hit the city.
   11. The students_____(speak) loudly and _____(not do) their work.
   12. I _____(ask) you questions and you_____(answer) them. Good work!

Exam practice: Reading part 4

B Read the following passage about popular tourist spots in Toronto and answer the questions Multiple choice questions can be difficult as many answers appear to be correct. Make sure you read the question carefully so that you know exactly what information you need to find.

Landmarks in Toronto

Casa Loma, (Spanish for Hill House) is a medieval style house in midtown Toronto that is now a museum and landmark. It was originally a residence for financier Sir Henry Mill Pellatt. In 1903, Sir Henry Pellatt purchased 25 lots and commissioned Canadian architect E.J. Lennox to design Casa Loma. Casa Loma was constructed by 300+ workers over a three-year period from 1911-1914 and cost 3.5 million to build. Building began with the stables, Potting Shed and Hunting Lodge a few hundred feet north of the main building.

At 98 rooms, it was the largest private residence in Canada. Notable amenities included an elevator, an oven large enough to cook an ox, 2 vertical passages for pipe organs, central vacuum, 2 secret passages in the ground floor office and three bowling alleys which were never completed. Most of the third floor was left unfinished and today serves as the Regimental Museum for the Queen's Own Rifles of Canada.

During World War II, Casa Loma was used to conceal research on sonar and for construction of sonar devices for U-boat detection. When the depression hit that followed World War 1, the City of Toronto increased Casa Loma's annual property taxes from $600 per year to $1,000 a month. In order to continue paying, $1.5 million in art and furnishings had to be auctioned for much less than they were worth. During the late 1920's, Casa Loma was also a popular nightspot but essentially remained vacant until 1933. The city eventually seized Casa Loma in 1933 for $27, 303 in back taxes.

The Canadian National Tower, or more commonly known, the CN Tower, is located downtown Toronto and is used for communications and observations. It is 553.33 metres tall and was completed in 1976. At that time, it was the world's tallest free-standing structure and tallest tower. It remained the tallest for 34 years but is currently the tallest in the Western Hemisphere only.

Construction began on February 6, 1973 and it was open to the public on June 26, 1976. It cost roughly $63 million and took nearly 1550 workers about 40 months to build. There were some dangerous moments during the construction but only one person is reported to have died during the entire construction process.

The CN Tower has 2 restaurants, a café, a gift shop and several attractions. The newest attraction is the Edgewalk, whereby visitors walk in groups of six around the perimeter of the Tower at a height of 1168 ft.

While Toronto boasts of having some fabulous buildings and structures, the Toronto Zoo is not to be missed. The Toronto Zoo opened August 15th, 1974 and is 710 acres in size. It is the largest zoo in Canada and is divided into 7 zoogeographic regions. These regions are Indo-Malaysia, Africa, Americas, Tundra Trek, Australasia, Eurasia and the Canadian Domain. The zoo is currently home to over 5,000 animals representing over 500 species.

The Toronto Zoo makes considerable effort to conserve endangered species from around the world. In order to operate a zoo of this size and care for all of the animals, the zoo employs more than 250 full time employees, 330 part time or seasonal workers and over 225 volunteers. One of the objectives of the zoo is to show not just the animals, but the animals in their native environments.

There are many future developments planned to improve and expand the current zoo facilities. These include the reintroduction of some exhibits, the introduction of new animals and exhibits and an Animal Health Centre. Currently on-site, you can find a variety of restaurants and cafes, a collection of rides and many retail stores.

If you go to Toronto, you can buy a cost effective CityPASS which will cover admission to these three attractions and more.

1. What do these tourist destinations have in common?
   a) They were all built in the 1970's
   b) They are all downtown Toronto
   c) They are part of a discount tourist pass
   d) They are the most popular attractions in Canada

2. Why were the taxes at Casa Loma raised?
   a) To pay for the development of sonar devices
   b) So the City could take Casa Loma for the Mayor to use
   c) Because the value of the land increased
   d) To generate City revenue during the depression

3. Which 2 attractions are the largest in their class?
   a) Casa Loma and the Toronto Zoo
   b) the CN Tower and the Toronto Zoo
   c) Casa Loma and the CN Tower
   d) All three are the largest in their class

4. What do Casa Loma and the CN Tower have in common?
   a) Both are historical structures
   b) Neither are owned by the City
   c) Both took less than 500 workers to complete
   d) Both took approximately 3 years to complete

5. Which attraction has a connection to the military?
   a) Casa Loma
   b) the CN Tower
   c) the Toronto Zoo
   d) None of the attractions are connected to the military

6. What does the Toronto Zoo try hard to do?
   a) Have a large variety of animals
   b) Save endangered species
   c) Employ the most people
   d) Breed as many animals as possible

Introduction to Writing exam: Practice including information and details needed

C Writing is a very important skill. We place a great deal of significance on writing in English. We are going to write a letter. Let's think about this situation.

You just came back from a holiday and you are not happy about the hotel you stayed in. You want to write a letter to the manager about the dirty room, the noisy guests next door, the bad food in the restaurant and the lack of towels for the swimming pool. Let's think about what we can say about these problems. We have to expand on our answers and give detail. Always plan before you write. Without planning, your writing will not be organized and you will not get a good mark on the exam. To get you started: how is the room dirty? Think of possible situations. Now do this for the other complaints you have. Use the space below to write down your ideas and plan.

1. Now that we have ideas, we can decide what we want to include. Check the question very carefully so you know exactly what you have to write about. For example, do you have to write about a problem or problems? Type your letter on a computer, turning the spellcheck function off and print it out. How long did it take? How many typing errors did you make?

 Grammar & Application: Activity collocations

D

When we talk about activities, we have to make sure we use the correct combination. Study these examples:

Go: swimming, running, golfing, climbing
Play: golf, tennis, baseball, hockey
Do: yoga, exercise, aerobics

Try to use these, but in the past forms (went, played, did). Have you ever had a really bad vacation? What about a really great vacation? Think about it for a minute and make some notes. You are going to tell your partner about it. You have to speak for 2 minutes if you can, so be sure to add lots of detail. To help you, look back at the interrogative pronouns in Unit 1 an use them as a guide when you are thinking about what you can say. For example: *Who? Who was with you. Where? Where did you go?*

The following listening activity is similar to a task you will have to complete on the exam. Being able to deduce or understand *implied* meaning is the ability to gain extra information from not only the words being used, but the tone of voice and words chosen.

In unit 3, we will practice some pronunciation tips and give you a guided lesson on how to increase your listening comprehension through understanding pronunciation patterns.

Introduction to Pronunciation: Assessing tone

E

1. You are going to hear a conversation between 2 friends talking about their recent vacations. As you listen, pay attention to their voices. Do they sound positive or negative? Do you get a good feeling or bad feeling? Make notes about what they say. When we are finished listening, you will have a minute to look at your notes and then you will give a brief summary of the conversation.

2. Now listen again and select the best sentences to describe what you heard.

1. A. The man had a great time
   B. The man spent a lot of time on the beach
   C. It rained every day
   D. The man took a lot of pictures

2. A. He didn't lay in the sun
   B. He laid in the sun for 15 minutes
   C. He feels rested when he lays in the sun
   D. He prefers to lay in the sun instead of taking pictures

3. A. The man put the pictures on social media
   B. The man is going to put the pictures on social media
   C. The man doesn't think people will like her pictures
   D. The man took too many pictures to put on social media

Exam practice: Reading part 3

Being able to identify the next word, logically, in a series of words or a sentence is a strong indication of your overall language ability. Read it through once to get the main idea then decide what kind of word you need to complete the sentence. Once you have identified what kind of word (noun, verb, adjective, etc.) it is easier to select a tone appropriate word.

F

The following text is missing some important words. The missing words could be prepositions, articles, verbs, etc.

Dragonboat racing [1] _____ one of the most amazing sports [2] _____ the world. Not [3] _____ is it a great team sport, but it is great exercise. Dragon boat racing is a Chinese traditional sport. There are 20 [4] _____ in the boat, one coxswain [5] _____ a drummer. Teams that do [6] _____ best are those that practice together to create synchronicity – everyone paddling at the [7] _____ time. It is a sheer adrenaline rush when you cross the [8] _____ line, with lactic acid rushing through your veins.

Every year, there are many regattas [9] _____ Canada. The Great White North event is [10] _____ in Toronto at Ontario Place and brings teams from across the country and [11] _____ the world. This event usually happens in September.

I remember my [12] _____ race. I was so excited and then so tired. The name of my team [13] _____ Nemesis. We merged with other teams to fill the [14] _____ for races and and traveled around Ontario [15] _____ the different regattas. Four of us even [16] _____ down to Fort Dodge, Iowa for a weekend of racing. That was an amazing trip. We met teams [17] _____ Ottawa, all over the States and even a [18] _____ from Britain.

Exam practice: Speaking part 3

The following exercises are similar to Part 3 of the Speaking exam. There are 3 possible tasks you will be asked to perform. All require a solid level of English. Leaving a voicemail, answering summary questions about a conversation and answering multiple questions about a news report. Your attention to detail and ability to understand key ideas will enable you to do well in this area.

A great way to prepare for this part of the exam and to improve your skills for your everyday experiences is to practice what you would say in different situations,
    a) making/cancelling a doctor appointment
    b) making/cancelling a hotel/restaurant reservation
    c) calling in sick
Other ideas include watching online news casts and making notes of main points, choose a news story and compare the information between networks; what is different?

G

1. Let's brainstorm about typical pieces of information we should include when we leave a voicemail. Sometimes, the information is the same for all kinds of voicemail and other times, the information is specific to the situation. Think about these questions:
    a) What do you say?
    b) How long should it be?
    c) What should you repeat?
    d) When would you leave a voicemail?

    Did you have a bad or awkward experience leaving a voicemail? What happened?

2. With a partner, imagine different situations and take turns leaving a voicemail. Then, present to the class for a group critique.

Always: Name	Situation 1: cancelling appointment	Situation 2: calling in sick

3. Listen carefully to the following news report and answer the accompanying questions..

    1. Name two ways pedestrians can be distracted.
    2. What three tips were given for crossing?
    3. How long do you have to cross the road?
    4. Did the reporter talk to Police?

    Were you in an accident before? Were you walking or driving? Describe the event to a partner.

Grammar: Past continuous and comparison to past simple

H

The past continuous is constructed the same way as the present continuous but uses the past form of be.

Let's examine: **was/were + ing** → I was sleeping. They were running. He was not eating.

Past simple and past continuous

We often use these 2 together when we are telling stories or recounting events. Knowing which verb to put into what form adds meaning and clarity. Don't forget sequencing words like **when, while, as.** Create a third example below.

1. I swam. A shark bit me.   2. I ate lunch. I listened to music.   3.

In these examples, we don't know the sequence of events or how they are related. We need to join the 2 actions and identify the time relationship.

We need to be careful how we join them though. Sometimes, only one sequence is acceptable. Other times, both ways are fine. For example: A shark was biting me while I swam. Does that make sense logically? Bite, bite, bite, again and again, while I enjoyed my swim? Clearly, we must clarify the swimming action as being continuous and the shark bite as interrupting! However, I was eating lunch while I listened to music **AND** I was listening to music while I ate lunch, are both fine, logically.

Application of past continuous and comparison to past simple

1. Create sentences using the 2 verbs given. Verbs are in infinitive form and must be changed. Decide how to put them together using both the past simple and past continuous. Some sentences can be constructed both ways. Don't forget to think logically!

    1. drive, listen to music
    2. eat chips, watch tv
    3. walk, see friend
    4. talk on phone, trip on curb
    5. have a bath, phone ring
    6. pour the milk, scare
    7. hold hat, wind blow
    8. fall, run
    9. take picture, not look
    10. wait, bite nails

2. Select 8 sentences and create 2 questions from the article in Unit 1, Part D about Calgary, and change them into the past. You can use both the past simple or the past continuous as appropriate. For example, *Calgary was a thriving city. Calgary got it's name from The Norse word kalt. Did others believe it came from Gaelic?*

    _____
    _____
    _____
    _____
    _____
    _____
    _____
    _____
    _____
    _____
    _____
    _____
    _____

3. Now share your sentences and questions with a partner and work together on correcting any mistakes. Write possible mistakes below and ask your teacher for clarification and explanation.

    _____
    _____
    _____
    _____
    _____
    _____
    _____
    _____
    _____

Review

Vocabulary to remember

Use this box to write any new vocabulary you learned in the unit

Write a short composition about a previous vacation using everything you have learned in the unit, adding as much information if you can. Think about activities, past simple and past continuous. Use positive and negative forms. Do not include questions.

Using your composition above, create comprehension questions using both interrogative questions and yes/no questions. Use the pronoun 'you' instead of 'I'.

Who are you?

Grammar: Subject/object pronouns and adjectives

A

1. Using the right pronoun or adjective is essential in English. Unlike gender-based languages, these extra words define the subject or object and give necessary information. You must memorize these until they become automatic. Take a moment to make sure you know the words in the box below and when to use them.

I	Me	My	Mine	Myself
You	You	Your	Yours	Yourself
He	Him	His	His	Himself
It	It	Its	----	Itself
She	Her	Her	Hers	Herself
We	Us	Our	Ours	Ourselves
They	Them	Their	Theirs	Themselves

2. As a group, try to think of as many words we use to describe people, based on gender, relationship, marital status, etc. as possible.

Male	Female	Both

Application of Subject/object pronouns and adjectives

3. Think of the people in your family, your friends, neighbours and classmates. Define their relationship to you or someone else. Write as many examples as you can think of using as many of the above. For example, *Daniel is my father and Mari is my mother. I am their daughter. They are my parents.*

_____
_____
_____
_____
_____
_____
_____
_____
_____
_____
_____
_____

Exam practice: Speaking part 2

Part 2 of the Speaking exam requires you to interpret either graphs or pictures. You will be shown a visual and will have to answer questions on what you see. The questions will only be given once and you will have 40 seconds to provide a complete response. There are a variety of scenarios that you could be asked to describe.

A great way to prepare for this part of the exam and to improve your skills for your everyday experiences is to scroll through your pictures or those of your friends on popular social media sites. Vacation photos are great as they include activities and new adventures to challenge your vocabulary skills!

B

1. Using the example as a guide, describe as many things as you can about what you see and try to infer or guess at context or emotions. Write your sentences in the space provided beside. You will then discuss with a partner what you see

There are 4 people in this picture. They are posing for the camera. They are siblings. There are 3 sons and one daughter. There are 3 men and one woman. She has 3 brothers. The men each have 2 brothers and one sister. One is sitting, two are standing and one is leaning. She has her arms around two of her brothers. One of her brothers has his arm around her waist. There is dirty truck behind them. They are outside. They look like they are a little bit tired because they are not smiling. Maybe they didn't win the mud race. They are outside and wearing big coats. Perhaps the weather is cool.

_____
_____
_____
_____
_____
_____

_____
_____
_____
_____
_____
_____

_____
_____
_____
_____
_____
_____

_____
_____
_____
_____
_____
_____

_____
_____
_____
_____
_____
_____

Exam practice: Listening part 5

This is similar to Part 5 of the listening exam. You will hear a conversation and you will have to answer questions on what you hear. On the exam, the questions will be multiple choice. You will have to infer the answers.

⭐ Follow the pronunciation queues that the speakers give. This will help you determine if they are finished speaking or if more information will be given. This is very helpful during an exam.

C

1. Listen to the following interview and answer the accompanying questions. Remember to listen fully before deciding.

    1. Where did he live in 1992?
    2. Does he have a large family?
    3. How many people are still living in his family?
    4. Does his sister work?
    5. Is his daughter still in high school?
    6. Is his daughter now in front of and behind the camera?
    7. How often does he see his family?
    8. Does he work in Ottawa often?

2. Now with a partner, create your own interview. Be sure to include pronunciation cues and the adjectives/pronouns in the pronunciation tips to the right. Use the space below to make notes.

Pronunciation Tips

English pronunciation is very musical. While there are many words in our sentences that are important for grammar, we generally don't place emphasis on 4 kinds of words.
a) Articles (a, an, the)
b) Prepositions (in, on, at, etc)
c) Auxiliary verbs (do, be, have, etc)
d) Conjunctions (and, but, so, etc)

By not emphasizing these words, we get an automatic high and low rhythm in a sentence and the content words are clear.

I **want** to **go** to **school**
I wasn't **told** of the **party** so I didn't **go**

Conversation cues include rising, falling and continuation tones.

Where do you live? ↘ This information question falls at the end
Did you enjoy your trip? ↗ This yes/no question rises at the end
When did you... → This incomplete question abruptly stops

Changes in the rhythm and tone occur for clarification and emphasis of specific points that depend on the mood and speaker.

No, not **on** the car. I said **in** the car.
I **really** dislike the idea **but** I will help you.

And finally, due to tone and intent being so important to convey messages in English, often words are misunderstood simply because the words and the tone don't match.

If in a sweet, kind voice, someone says "That's the ugliest dress I have ever seen", the listener would be confused. Likewise, while using a flat or rude tone, if someone says " I'd love to help you move', the listener would assume the speaker was being sarcastic.

Part 4 of the listening exam requires you to infer intent and tone from a dialogue. Listen carefully to the tone and to the words and follow the cues.

Introduction to Listening part 4

D

1. Why do people communicate? As a group, think about why we exchange words with each other. To start you off, here are some reasons. Think as many as you can.

    - Give advice
    - Make a demand
    - Ask a question

2. Listen to the following dialogues and determine the purpose of their communication.

1.	6.
2.	7.
3.	8.
4.	9.
5.	10.

Exam practice: Reading part 4

E Read the following passage about Regina and answer the questions. Make sure you read the question carefully so that you know exactly what information you need to find.

Queen City of the Plains

Regina is the capital city of Saskatchewan. It was named for Queen Victoria who was the Queen of England when Regina was incorporated in 1882. "Regina" is the Latin word for "queen," and so to this day the city is known as the "Queen City of the Plains."

While its name speaks of pageantry and royalty, the city's first name was much less glamorous: Pile of Bones. That's what it was originally known as, the name derived from the huge pile of buffalo bones that accumulated there as the prairie buffalo herds, sometimes numbering in the hundreds of thousands, were hunted by First Nations people, the original inhabitants of the area. Regina was named the capital city of Saskatchewan following the province's entry into Canadian confederation in 1905. It's as a capital city that the city really finds its beauty and asserts its identity.

Regina is set in the middle of the Canadian prairie, which is one of the flattest places on the planet. Regina owes much of its identity and prosperity to the farming that takes place all around it. At one time this region was known as "the breadbasket of the world" and to this day wheat, flax and more recently soy crops thrive in the rich soil, under the dazzling prairie sun. A trip just outside of town reveals the beautiful dome of the sky and on a summer's day, high white clouds drifting by that have earned Saskatchewan the name of "land of the living skies."

Regina is also known as the "Home of the RCMP," and is the location of the world-famous police force's training depot, where it has been training officers since 1885. There is a chapel on the grounds that dates back to the 1880's, the time of the North West Mounted Police. The RCMP museum houses many fascinating artifacts, including a length of the rope used to hang Metis leader Louis Riel, who was executed for treason in Regina in 1885 – one of the most contentious and divisive events in Canadian history.

1. According to the article, how many names, past and present, does Regina have?
   a) 2
   b) 3
   c) 4
   d) 5

2. Who originally named Regina?
   a) First Nations people
   b) The Latins
   c) The people of Saskatchewan
   d) The Queen of England

3. What riches does the area offer?
   a) soy, bread, sun
   b) sun, soy, wheat
   c) blue sky, sun, bread
   d) soy, wheat, flax

4. What does the article say about the RCMP?
   a) They are all from Regina
   b) They train there
   c) In 1885, RCMP were trained there
   d) The RCMP are famous

5. What happened to Louis Riel?
   a) He was executed for treason
   b) He was hung at the RCMP museum
   c) The Metis hung him for treason
   d) Regina killed him with rope

Exam practice: Reading part 3

F The following text is missing some important words. The missing words could be prepositions, articles, verbs, etc.

Much of Regina's political, cultural, intellectual and recreational activities [1]_____ place in facilities located [2]_____ Wascana Park. At 9.3 square km, the park is [3]_____ larger than either New York's Central Park [4]_____ Stanley Park in Vancouver. There are many government buildings, [5]_____ the legislature and the T.C. Douglas building – named for the Saskatchewan premier [6]_____ championed universal medicare that all Canadians now enjoy – which contains [7]_____ Norman MacKenzie Art Gallery. Both campuses of the University of Regina [8]_____ located in Wascana Park, as are the Saskatchewan Centre of the Arts, The Royal Saskatchewan Museum, the Saskatchewan Science Centre and many [9]_____ popular attractions. Wascana Lake itself is a centre for rowing and other aquatic activities in the [10]_____ and skating and cross-country skiing [11]_____ the winter.

Grammar: Talking about the future

G

We have no specific future tense in English. To create a future meaning, we use the present tense and add words that represent the future. Some of these words are referred to as modal verbs others are simply time words. Also, we can use the present continuous form with a future time word.

Let's examine:

I will call you tomorrow	I can call you later
I may not need your help	I have to see the doctor
I'm going skiing tomorrow	I should go home soon
I'm not making dinner tonight	I must not forget

Application of the future

1. Write a brief composition about what you plan on having for dinner, what you are going to do on the weekend, your plans for summer or Christmas holiday or what you will do once you become a Permanent Resident in Canada. Use a variety of grammatical forms. Use the space below to make some notes before you begin.

2. Read the following text and answer the questions.

Every year we have our family reunion in a quaint little stone building at a place called Harrison Park. We have held our reunion there for many years and it is a real treat to see everyone. Often times people travel from all over Canada to attend the annual event. It is a great opportunity to catch up with family and extended family and to reconnect. Everyone brings a dish to contribute to the potluck feast and several activities are planned. Every year, one or two people volunteer to host and they are responsible for the activities, games, theme, date, booking and reminders. This year we will be celebrating several anniversaries, birthdays and various life events. The theme is going to be centered around "Milestones" and should be great fun! Because it is held in a park during the summer, we will probably play baseball or simply throw a Frisbee or ball around. Some are going to bring their bathing suits to swim in the pool while others are happy to walk around the park and look at the wonderful variety of birds that choose the park as their home. I am looking forward to seeing everyone!

1. Why do they get together?

2. How often do they get together?

3. Where do they go?

4. What is the theme going to be?

5. What will they be celebrating?

6. What activities will they probably do?

Exam practice: Writing part 1

You will be given a situation to respond to with guidelines and clear instructions on what you have to include. Make sure you fully read the question so you don't leave anything out. 125 well organized and correctly used words is your goal. Avoid repetition and make sure you stay on topic.

Make sure you plan before you write. It is essential for you to develop your ideas BEFORE you start writing. Simply throwing ideas together into a text will not get you a good mark. Make idea generation part of your preparation before you start. Organization and clarity are just as important as grammar and spelling.

H

Write a letter (100-125 words) to a family member that you have recently seen at a family reunion. Include :
i. Expressions of happiness to have seen them
ii. Gratitude for organizing such a great time
iii. Ask for pictures
iv. Invite them to your house for a holiday

Review

Vocabulary to remember

Use this box to write any new vocabulary you learned in the unit

Write a short composition about your family using everything you have learned in the unit, adding as much information as you can. Think about people, relationships, activities, present, past and future simple and continuous. Use positive and negative forms. Do not include questions.

Using your composition above, create comprehension questions using both interrogative questions and yes/no questions. Use the pronoun 'you' instead of 'I' where applicable.

When is dinner?

Grammar: Countable/uncountable nouns and articles

A

There are two kinds of nouns in English: those we can count and those we can't. When we can count a noun, changing it from singular to plural is easy.

Let's examine: 1 cat   5 cat**s**   1 city   5 cit**ies**   1 box   5 box**es**

Nouns that are uncountable need a count word added. Notice the addition of the word **of**:
  1 **bottle of** water   5 **bottles of** water   1 **cup of** sugar   5 **cups of** sugar

In these examples, water and sugar are uncountable nouns.. You can often logically decide which are countable and which aren't. If you think about counting each hair on a person's head...that seems impossible. Or counting each grain of rice or molecule of sugar? Can you think of other count words for uncountable nouns? Write them below.

We use **a/an/the** instead of numbers with nouns. These articles represent 1(one) We use **a** before hard consonants *(car, hotel, boat)*, **an** before soft vowel sounds *(apple, hour, umbrella)*. We use **the** before superlatives *(the best, the biggest, the most modern)* and when there is only one in the world, a group known as one or it is unique *(the sun, the Rocky Mountains, the United Kingdom)*

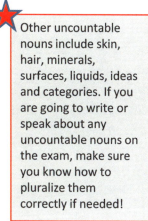

Other uncountable nouns include skin, hair, minerals, surfaces, liquids, ideas and categories. If you are going to write or speak about any uncountable nouns on the exam, make sure you know how to pluralize them correctly if needed!

Application of Countable/uncountable nouns and articles

1. Look at the following words and decide if they are countable or uncountable. If they are uncountable, think of words we can use to count them.

   money: uncountable; bags, wads, dollars, pounds, yen etc.

   toast

   salt

   milk

   fish

   corn

   sweat

   candy

   chocolate

   aspirin

   grocery

   soil

   luggage

2. The following text is missing articles. Insert a/an/the or no article (-) as appropriate

   _____ Food is _____ essential for all _____ living things to survive. Some people simply eat _____ food to live while others live to eat food! There are _____ many varieties of food to choose from. Fresh food includes _____ fruit and _____ vegetables, _____ fish and some _____ meat. Processed food includes _____ convenient ready-made dinners and _____ junk food, as well as sauces and items in _____ jars and boxes. In Canada, _____ steak and vegetables are very popular. _____ nutrition we get from food is not only _____ very important for _____ healthy body, but for _____ healthy mind. If you don't have enough _____ healthy food in your _____ diet, you will probably feel _____ fatigued.

29

B

1. You are going to hear a recipe and directions on how to make a particular dish. You will hear several articles and sequencing words (first, next, etc.). Listen carefully and write down the sequencing words you hear. You will need to use these later.

> ⭐ Using sequencing words correctly will increase your overall mark on the writing exam. There are a variety of ways to sequence events, not only 'firstly,' 'secondly,' etc

C Think about and make notes for the following questions and then discuss with a partner.

What is your favourite food?
What is your favourite meal?
Is it healthy?
How often do you eat it?
How long does it take to make?
What is it called in your language?
Who introduced it to you?
Why do you like it?
What is your favourite restaurant? Why?

Vocabulary: Food descriptions, categories and collocations

D

1. Give examples for each of the following adjectives describing food. Think as many as you can and then share with the class.

Sour: *old milk, lemons, limes*
Rotten:
Spicy:
Rancid:
Sweet:
Bland:
Burnt:
Stale:
Bitter:
Ripe:
Fresh:
Cholesterol Free:
Gritty:
Acidic:
Fluffy:

2. There are many categories of food. Do you know them? After making sure you know what they mean, decide if they are good ⬆ or bad ⬇ for you.

Protein ⬆ ⬇
Carbohydrates ⬆ ⬇
Fat ⬆ ⬇
Vegetables ⬆ ⬇
Fruit ⬆ ⬇
Grains ⬆ ⬇
Dairy ⬆ ⬇

> What can we *make*? *breakfast, lunch, dinner, a meal, a snack, a feast*
> List other things we can make.
>
> When do we use *have* and *go*? *have a party, go for dinner*
> List other uses of have and go.

Application of new vocabulary

3. Using the pronunciation help from unit 3, create a dialogue with a partner at a restaurant. Discuss the menu and place your order. Be sure to include food descriptions and various tones and intonations. For example, maybe the waiter didn't hear you, so you need to adjust your intonation for clarification.

Exam practice: Reading part 2

The following exercise is similar to Part 2 of the Reading exam. You will be required to analyze and answer questions relating to a graph or table of information. Be careful to extract the exact info you need by focusing on the questions that need answered. In many instances, there is much more information than you need to understand.

Understand the questions you are being asked clearly. Identify the main points of the question and slowly, by process of elimination, zero in on the exact information you have been requested to find. Multiple choice questions can be difficult so pay extra attention to the differences between the possible answers.

E Look at the following tables of information and answer the questions that follow.

	Children			Teens		Adults			
	2-3	4-8	9-13	14-18 Years		19-50 Years		51+ Years	
	Girls and Boys			Female	Male	Female	Male	Female	Male
Vegetables and Fruit	4	5	6	7	8	7-8	8-10	7	7
Grain Products	3	4	6	6	7	6-7	8	6	7
Milk and Alternatives	2	2	3-4	3-4	3-4	2	2	3	3
Meat and Alternatives	1	1	1-2	2	3	2	3	2	3

	Females				Males		
Age	Sedentary Level	Low Active Level	Active Level	Age	Sedentary Level	Low Active Level	Active Level
2-3 y	1100	1250	1400	2-3 y	1100	1350	1500
4-5 y	1200	1350	1500	4-5 y	1250	1450	1650
6-7 y	1300	1500	1700	6-7 y	1400	1600	1800
8-9 y	1400	1600	1850	8-9 y	1500	1750	2000
10-11 y	1500	1800	2050	10-11 y	1700	2000	2300
12-13 y	1700	2000	2250	12-13 y	1900	2250	2600
14-16 y	1750	2100	2350	14-16 y	2300	2700	3100
17-18 y	1750	2100	2400	17-18 y	2450	2900	3300
19-30 y	1900	2100	2350	19-30 y	2500	2700	3000
31-50 y	1800	2000	2250	31-50 y	2350	2600	2900
51-70 y	1650	1850	2100	51-70 y	2150	2350	2650
71 y +	1550	1750	2000	71 y +	2000	2200	2500

http://www.hc-sc.gc.ca/fn-an/food-guide-aliment/basics-base/1_1_1-eng.php

1. 10 year old children should have how many servings per day of vegetables and fruit, grain, milk and meat?
   a) 6, 6, 1-2, 3-4   b) 6, 6, 3-4, 1-2   c) 7, 6, 3-4, 2   d) 5, 4, 2, 1

2. Teen boys should have how many servings per day of vegetables and fruit, grain, milk and meat?
   a) 7, 6, 3-4, 2   b) 7-8, 6-7, 2, 2   c) 7, 8, 3, 3-4   d) 8, 7, 3-4, 3

3. Women over 50 should consume how many servings per day of vegetables and fruit, grain, milk and meat?
   a) 7, 6, 3, 2   b) 6, 7, 2, 3   c) 7, 7, 3, 3   d) 7-8, 6-7, 2, 2

4. The sedentary level of caloric intake for females aged 14-16 is the same as

a) There is no equivalent male level
b) The sedentary male aged 51-70
c) The low activity level of boys aged 8-9
d) The low activity level of men aged 51-70

5. The highest caloric intake listed for males is

a) 900 more per day than females
b) 2200 more per day than females
c) 3 times more than for females
d) There is no equivalent for females

6. The highest amount of calories per day for low activity females is

a) 2100 and spans 18 years
b) 2400 and is for 17-18 year olds
c) 2100 and only for teenagers
d) 2100 and spans 3 decades

F The following text is similar to those found on the reading exam. Using the previous questions you have answered as a guide, make 6 multiple choice questions for the text below. Try to think about possible questions that might be associated with this kind of text. You will then share your questions with the class. As stated before, if you can produce examples of what you are trying to learn, you know you have made progress.

A cold, tiny spot

Up at the top of Canada, on the southern shore of Ellesmere Island, we find the tiny community of Grise Fiord – Canada's northern most community – with a population of around 100 people. The hamlet lies 1,160 km north of the Arctic Circle, and some 3,500 km north of Ottawa. It is one of the coldest communities in the world, with an average yearly temperature of -16 degrees C. The people who inhabit this small, remote community have traditionally been referred to as "eskimoes," but nowadays we know that they are members of the Inuit nation, and so we refer to them as such. The word "Inuit" can be translated as "the people."

In the winter, because it is located so far north, the sun never rises above the horizon. For a brief period of time in the summer, the sun never sets, which explains why the high Arctic is sometimes referred to as "the land of the midnight sun."

The Arctic, because it is most often shrouded in darkness, and the temperature remains well below freezing, has very little vegetation. The diet of the Inuit people was therefore traditionally very different than that of people virtually anywhere else in the world. With no access to fruit or vegetables, the inhabitants of the high Arctic had to get all of their nutrition from animals, including musk oxen, seals, whales, caribou and arctic char. In particular, their diet and their health depended on the internal organs as well as the fat of these animals.

Grise Fiord is not a traditional or indigenous settlement. When Canada's northern-most territories, such as Ellesmere Island, came under international dispute, the Canadian Government thought that a community on the disputed island would strengthen Canada's case for its sovereignty, and so the community was created.

Grise Fiord features services and amenities that one would expect to find in any community such as a school and a nursing station and police services. There is also a Co-op store that sells everything that inhabitants of the community could want, including food. The presence of this store caused a shift in the diet of the people, from their traditional meat-based diet to more of a mixed "southern" fare.

Ironically, this has led to more problems than it has solved. Food that has to be transported so far is very expensive. Less healthy food tends to travel better than food that is good for us. The introduction of sugar and carbohydrates to their diet has left the people in poorer overall health than they were on their traditional diet, proving that sometimes progress is a subjective term.

1.

a)
b)
c)
d)

2.

a)
b)
c)
d)

3.

a)
b)
c)
d)

4.

a)
b)
c)
d)

5.

a)
b)
c)
d)

6.

a)
b)
c)
d)

G

Describe how the diet of your native country is affected by climate? Geography? Cultural factors? Has it changed? In what way? Would you be able to live on a diet completely void of fruit and vegetable? What would be the hardest for you to give up? Take a moment to make some notes and write down some ideas

You are going to create a news item describing what affects diets. Develop your information from above into complete sentences. Working with a partner, combine your ideas and decide who will say what. Create 4 questions to accompany your news article for the other students in your class. You will each need to speak for 1 minute minimum.

Review

Vocabulary to remember

Use this box to write any new vocabulary you learned in the unit

---

Think of your favourite food and write the recipe below. Be sure to include sequencing words we heard in exercise B and include all steps.

Using your recipe above, think of descriptive words to use for the food you have mentioned. Pretend you are on a food program and you have to encourage other people to make this at home. *This is such a delicious dish. Very savoury and it melts in your mouth.* You will be presenting your descriptions to the class!

How long have you been here?

Grammar: Perfect tenses

A

The perfect tenses allow us to talk about the past and the present and make assumptions about the future all in one sentence.

have/has + past participle   **have/has + been + ing**   **had + past participle**   **had + been + ing**

As you can see, we continue to follow the rules of forming the continuous (be + ing) when creating the present or past perfect continuous forms. Be careful not to confuse 'been' with 'being' as they can sometimes sound similar in some sentences depending on the speakers pronunciation.

What is the difference between the simple and perfect tenses?

Life events and experiences are not fixed points. Our actions span time, starting and stopping at different times even overlapping each other. The simple tenses focus on the events at a particular time. The perfect tenses focus on the time and the relationship of the events. Simply put, the focus is different.

Let's examine these 2 sentences. Can you identify the shift in focus? Discuss as a group and think of more examples to compare

She went to Portugal for the first time 10 years ago.   She has been going to Portugal every winter since 2003

Application of Perfect tenses

1. Create sentences using the information given. Verbs can be in any form and must be changed. Sometimes, more than one form is possible. Use time phrases, question and negative forms and a variety of subjects as appropriate. Write as many forms as you can logically and be prepared to explain the difference in meaning.

   1. Live, 4 countries: I have lived in 4 countries. *This means I might live in more in the future*. I lived in 4 countries last year. *This means last year, I moved 4 different times to 4 different countries.*

   2. Cook, this morning

   3. Have accident, visit family

   4. 30 minutes, swim

   5. Have, 6 jobs

   6. Package, arrive yet

   7. Play tennis, 7 years old

   8. Hike, last summer

   9. Take 5000 pictures, this vacation

   10. Gain weight, break leg

2. Read this brief article about the naming and current status of Ottawa. Circle the correct tense. The first one has been done for you.

In 1826, Colonel John By 1 *named*/*had named* the area around the Rideau Canal Bytown. Within 30 years, it 2 *grew/had grown* substantially and it 3 *became/had become* clear this would eventually grow into a great city. In 1855, Bytown was incorporated as a City and they 4 *changed/had changed* the name to Ottawa. This name 5 *comes from/has come from* the Algonquin language, meaning "to trade." In 1857, Queen Victoria 6 *asked/had been asked* to choose a capital and she 7 *chose/had chosen* Ottawa as the capital of the "province of Canada". This was in part because it 8 *lies/has been lying* about halfway between the capitals of French and English Canada, Quebec City and Toronto, respectively.

Today, Ottawa is not only the capital city of Canada, but it is also the centre of many high-tech industries. It 9 *grew/has grown* to be Canada's sixth largest city, and 10 *ranks/has ranked* high in quality of life surveys for many years. It is said to have the second highest quality of living of any North American city, and 11 *has been ranked/has been ranking* as the third cleanest city in the world. In many surveys it 12 *holds/has held* the status of the best community in Canada to live in.

Exam practice: Reading part 1

> You will be given a letter to read. Once you have read the letter, you will have several True/False questions to answer. Make sure you read the letter and the questions carefully so that you don't make any unnecessary mistakes.

> ★ A great way to practice for this part of the exam is to create your own True/False questions with newspaper articles and emails. It will improve your comprehension skills as well as increase your speed

B Read the following letter and answer the accompanying True/False questions

Dear Alice,

I've been having such a great time here in Ottawa! I can't believe I have never been here before. That is just crazy. Anyway, the weather has been beautiful, which is super because I love walking around the city.

It's probably safe to say that I've never felt quite as Canadian as I have since visiting Ottawa. We will have to come here together some day. I know you would love it; it is quite beautiful and regal looking. The centre of the city is dominated by Parliament Hill, which has at its centre, the elegant Peace Tower. Behind the Peace Tower and the Centre Block of Parliament, where, as you know, the governance of the country takes place, I found the beautiful Library of Parliament. While the original Parliament buildings burned to the ground in 1916, the Parliamentary Library was saved, leaving it as the oldest and only original building left on Parliament Hill.

I am very surprised by the Rideau Canal. I have seen numerous pictures, but never imagined it to be so breathtaking in person. Not only are the walkways and parks filled with green spaces and littered with flowers but it has such a peaceful atmosphere about it.

Yesterday, I visited the Byward Market and was astounded by the variety of items and sheer size! Did you know it covers 4 blocks and has everything from boutiques and cafes to hair salons and restaurants? I have picked up a present for you.

See you soon,
Lucy

1. Lucy is enjoying her trip — True/False
2. Lucy thinks Ottawa is crazy — True/False
3. Alice feels Canadian in Ottawa — True/False
4. Lucy and Alice are going to go back to Ottawa together — True/False
5. The Library of Parliament burned to the ground — True/False
6. Parliament Hill is the oldest building in Ottawa — True/False
7. There is a lot of garbage along the canal — True/False
8. Lucy purchased a present for Alice — True/False

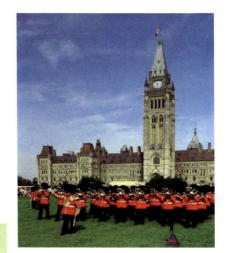

Exam practice: Reading part 4

C Read the following text and answer the multiple choice questions that follow

Capital Beauty

Ottawa is the home of many museums and galleries, including the National Gallery of Canada. The National Gallery houses a treasure of Canadian art, with extensive collections of such iconic artists as Tom Thomson, The Group of Seven, Emily Carr, Alex Colville and other artists from Canada and the rest of the world.

The Canadian Museum of Civilization is another significant museum in the National Capital Region. This museum, while now housed in a beautiful facility across the Ottawa River from Parliament Hill, has been identified as one of North America's oldest cultural institutions, dating back to 1856. It houses artifacts that reflect and celebrate the cultural diversity of Canada and its people.

The establishment of Ottawa, or Bytown as it was then known, had to do with the construction of the Rideau Canal. This canal was constructed during the War of 1812 to bypass the St. Lawrence River where it borders on New York State. Today the canal has been designated as a UNESCO World Heritage Site. In August, it is the site of the Rideau Canal Festival and in winter it has been called "the world's largest skating rink."

The historical notion of Bytown has been kept alive in Ottawa with the presence of the Byward Market, which was established by Colonel John By back in 1826 as a public market and gathering place.

1. What museums and galleries can be found in Ottawa?
   a) National Gallery of Canada, The Canadian Museum of Civilization, Parliament Hill, Bytown Market
   b) National Gallery of Canada, The Canadian Museum of Civilization
   c) National Gallery of Canada, The Canadian Museum of Civilization, Rideau Canal Festival
   d) National Gallery of Canada, The Canadian Museum of Civilization, Bytown Market

2. What can we find in the National Gallery of Canada?
   a) Works of art by only Canadian artists
   b) Works of art by both Canadian and international artists
   c) Gold and other valuable items
   d) Cultural and educational documents only

3. What was said about the Canadian Museum of Civilization?
   a) It is the oldest building in North America
   b) It is a house across from Parliament Hill
   c) You can find art and facts there
   d) You can find many cultural pieces of art there

4. What happens in August?
   a) It becomes a World Heritage site
   b) The Rideau Canal Festival
   c) You can skate on the canal
   d) It is used instead of the St. Lawrence River

5. What does it say about Byward Market?
   a) It is a hospital
   b) It was for the army
   c) It was built in 1826
   d) It is an old building

Exam practice: Speaking part 4

 You will be required to respond to a question. Your oral response to a topic will be graded based on your ability to speak clearly, concisely and with fluency. The question could be about any subject. You will be given 2 minutes, so take a few moments to make some notes BEFORE you begin speaking. Be careful not to repeat yourself and avoid random 'thinking noises' (uhhhh, hmmmm, aaannnnd ummmm)

★ A fantastic way to practice for this type of question is to record yourself responding to different topics in day to day life. Listen to yourself and critique your speed, your rhythm, use of grammar and any thinking noises you make. Try again to check your progress. You will be surprised how effective this can be!

D

1. Look at the following 3 questions. Prepare some notes for each question. Working with a partner who will time you, take turns speaking for about 2 minutes. Help each other to correct any errors or ways to improve and try again. How much did you improve?

   1. Nearly everyone has a 'bucket list' or list of things they want to do in their life. What is something you have always wanted to try?

   2. Happiness comes in many forms. What do you believe to be the most important factors in life to make us happy?

   3. Traveling around the world and visiting other countries can open one's mind. How valuable do you believe traveling to be?

   What errors did you make? What do you want to improve? List your errors here.

Grammar: Conditionals (*if* and *when* sentences)

E

What do we use conditionals for? Look at these examples and decide what their purpose is. What are they expressing? What is the time? We can express facts, things we strongly believe will happen, things we doubt will happen, regret, a desire to change the past, speculating about a different past. Many of these refer to hypothetical situations.

If you do not drink water, you will die
If I won the lottery, I would buy a new house
When I turn 68, I might retire
When I come to town, we should get together

If I win the lottery, I will buy a new house
If I had won the lottery, I wold have bought a new house
I would have called if I had known you were home
If I knew, I would tell you

Notice how we change the tense of the verbs used, depending on our perspective and the time? Every language has the same function of communicating the hypothetical, expressing dreams and regrets and stating factual conditions. Familiarize yourself with the verb changes and constructions of this in English and you will be well on your way to having deeper and more comprehensive conversations with your friends.

Application of Conditionals (*if* and *when* sentences)

1. Create 10 conditional sentences. Use the previous units in this book and the various topics to give you ideas. Identify the purpose or use of your sentence. You can also talk about true hypothetical situations in your life. For example, *If I pass this exam, I can get my Permanent Residency in Canada. This is a fact.*

   1. _____

   2. _____

   3. _____

   4. _____

   5. _____

   6. _____

   7. _____

   8. _____

   9. _____

   10. _____

2. Working in a group, discuss your ideas and sentences above. Going back to unit 1, create follow up questions after listening to the other students in your group. Use the interrogative pronouns from Unit 1 to help you. For example, *If I had known Ottawa was so beautiful, I would have moved there from my country. Why do you think Ottawa is so beautiful?*

Review

Vocabulary to remember

Use this box to write any new vocabulary you learned in the unit

Think about your city or your country and create a composition about it. Maybe there are special areas of the city or festivals. Include various perfect tenses and other tenses as appropriate. Do not include any conditional sentences.

Using your composition above, about your city or country, create conditional sentences. For example, *If you go to Byward Market, you can buy presents for people and have your hair done.*

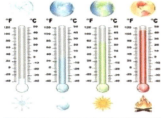

Why is it so warm?

Grammar: Comparatives and superlatives

A

When we want to talk about the differences between things or the ways they are the same, we use the **comparative**. The construction of comparatives is quite easy to remember.
Start with your adjective. There are 3 main changes to think about: **er, ier, more/less**
small – small**er**
quiet - quiet**er**
happy – happ**ier**
comfortable – **more** comfortable, **less** comfortable

Small is a one-syllable word. With most one-syllable words, we add **er**
Quiet is a two-syllable word. We can also add **er**.
Happy is a two-syllable word and it ends in **–y** so, we have to change that **-y** to **i** before we add **er**
Comfortable is a three-syllable word. "Comfortabler" sounds strange, right? So, instead, add **more/less**
Don't forget about the irregular forms like good – **better** and bad – **worse**. We use the word **than** to connect the things we are comparing.

I love Vancouver. I think Vancouver is a very friendly city. I think Vancouver is **friendlier than** Edmonton. I think Vancouver is **the friendliest** city in Canada.

The **superlative** is used when we want to talk about one thing and its position or rank.
Notice how we use **'the'** with the superlative? We do this because we are talking about one thing (one city, one idea, one bar, etc.) or one group of things (one class of students, one group of friends, etc)
Again, start with your adjective. There are 3 main changes: **est, iest, the most/the least**
small – **the smallest**
quiet – **the quietest**
happy – **the happiest**
the most comfortable, **the least** comfortable

Other forms include: **more** pollution **than**, not **as much** pollution **as**, **the least** pollution, a great deal **more** pollution **than**, a considerable amount **less** pollution **than**, **larger and larger**, **more** and **more** expensive

Application of Comparatives and superlatives

1. Complete the following sentences with the comparative or superlative as appropriate. Don't forget *than, as-as*, and *not* when necessary.

   1. Cities are _____ (big) they were 200 years ago.
   2. Canada's population is _____ (not large) Poland's population.
   3. Buildings that are downtown are _____ (much, tall) those that are located in the suburbs.
   4. Computers are _____ (modern) typewriters.
   5. Traffic was crazy today. The roads were _____ (a lot, congested) normal.
   6. Buses aren't _____ (convenient) a personal car.
   7. Glaciers are melting _____ (much, faster) scientists originally thought.
   8. Which country has_____ (good) environmental plan?
   9. The topic of the environment is becoming _____ (more, important)
   10. What is _____ (long) river in the world?

2. Now create sentences of your own using the various forms just covered

1.

2.

3.

4.

5.

Exam practice: Listening part 3

  You will be required to identify similar meanings. You will hear a recorded statement and you will have to choose which one of four sentences is closest in meaning. You will only hear the recording once. This part of the exam specifically tests your knowledge of synonyms and expressions that communicate the same or similar meaning.

★ Thesauruses are a fantastic resource for vocabulary building. For example, if you look up the word *big*, you will find numerous synonyms. Some can be interchangeable in a sentence while others are context specific. *Vast*, for example means big but has a limited use: *The Saraha is a vast desert*. We cannot say: *I have a vast chair.*

B
1. Listen to the recorded sentences and select the statement that BEST matches what you hear in the recording.

1. a) Vancouver doesn't have any major highways.
   b) Vancouver is the only city without highways downtown.
   c) Vancouver is not cut in half by a highway.
   d) Major highways are located outside of Vancouver's city centre

2. a) There are plenty of ways to reduce climate change.
   b) Action on climate change depends on where you live.
   c) There are many solutions that fix climate change.
   d) There are plenty of ways to stop climate change

3. a) Vancouver is the highest ranked environmental city internationally.
   b) Vancouver is well liked by millions of people.
   c) Vancouver ranks highly in international environmental surveys.
   d) Vancouver has the most environmental initiatives internationally.

4. a) Vancouver has a big park in the middle.
   b) There are several parks around Vancouver.
   c) Many people visit Vancouver parks.
   d) Vancouver is known for the amount of green areas throughout the city

5. a) Most of the original businesses in Vancouver dealt with logging.
   b) Large logging companies were the only businesses in early Vancouver.
   c) Large logging companies took over the economy in Vancouver.
   d) The economy in Vancouver is mostly driven by logging.

6. a) David Suzuki won an award for his environmental work.
   b) David Suzuki is a well known Canadian advocate for environmental issues.
   c) A Canadian environmental award was given to a famous person.
   d) David Suzuki is a famous Canadian who talks a lot about the environment.

7. a) No other Canadian city is as warm as Vancouver.
   b) There are other cities in Canada that are just as warm as Vancouver.
   c) There are no warm cities in Canada except Vancouver.
   d) Vancouver is the warmest city in Canada.

8. a) UBC is the best university in the world.
   b) UBC is the 40th best university in the world.
   c) Out of 40, UBC always ranks as one of the best in the world.
   d) UBC is the best university in Canada.

Vocabulary: Talking about the environment

C Match the words on the left with a word on the right. The first one has been done for you.

1. greenhouse   a) fuels
2. ozone   b) fumes
3. melting   c) power
4. exhaust   d) ice caps
5. renewable   e) species
6. eco   f) layer
7. fossil   g) effect
8. solar, wind, tidal h) energy
9. space   i) junk
10. endangered   j) friendly

D What kind of natural disasters can affect the environment? List as many as you can. Two examples have been given to start you off.

Floods
Drought

Talking about the environment

E In small groups, discuss the following questions.

1. How has climate change affected your country?
2. Is it warmer? Colder? Dryer? Wetter?
3. What do you do to help the environment?
4. Do you think that it is the government's responsibility to protect the environment?
5. What worries you the most about the environment?

Vocabulary: Technology and the environment

1. There are many inventions that are good for the environment, however, there are also numerous advancements that are not. Thinking about items we use every day, energy generation, inventions, buildings, new and old methods of farming and manufacturing, etc, complete the chart below. A few examples have been provided to get you started.

Bad for the environment	Good for the environment
Cars – gasoline & diesel	*Electric/hybrid cars*
Factories	*Recycling stations*
Sea ports	*Nature reserves*

Application of technology and the environment and general environmental vocabulary

1. You are the leader of a new civilization. You have any and all available technology to use. Think about where your people will work, live, play. How they will travel, what they will eat, where their garbage will go. What about import and export and electricity or alternative energy? Once you have created your new civilization, you will have to present and explain your decisions. Make sure to include as much information from this unit as possible and look back through the other units for grammar and vocabulary as appropriate.

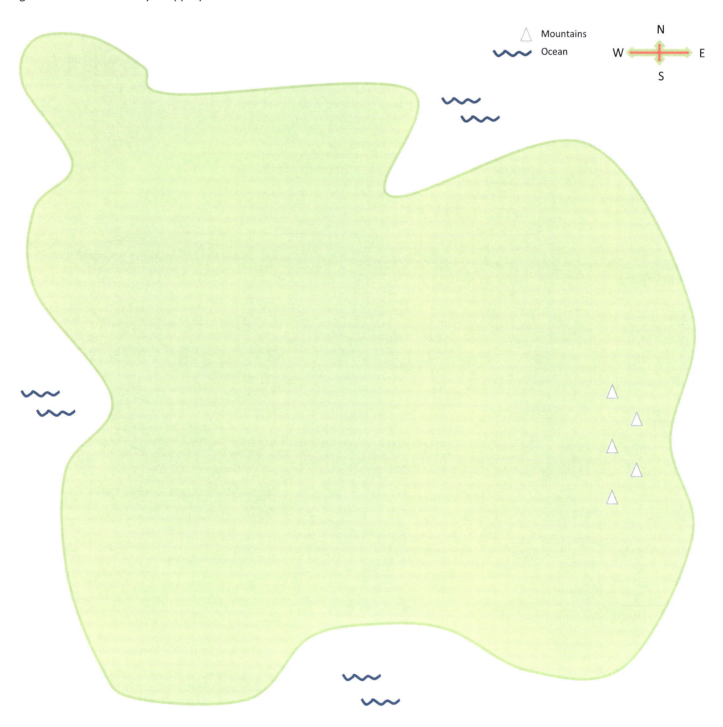

Review

Vocabulary to remember

Use this box to write any new vocabulary you learned in the unit

---

Think about the civilization you have just created. How is it better than your current city? How is it similar? Write a composition describing the environmental benefits of your civilization and compare and contrast it in as many ways as possible. For example: *My current city has several places for people to drop of recycling but not everyone recycles. In my civilization, people get paid when they recycle, so everyone does.*

Using your composition above, your civilization and the vocabulary in this unit, create 5 actions that you would do to help the environment in your current city. For example, *I would not allow high powered boats on the river because it destroys the habitat of the fish.*

How much is that?

Grammar: Conjunctions

A

The function of a conjunction is to group information. The information can be positive or negative. The conjunction you use depends on how you are putting the information together and what your purpose is.

And - to add additional information — *I bought shoes **and** socks when I went shopping today*
But – to add an opposing point — *I bought shoes **but** I forgot to buy socks*
So (that) – to give a result or purpose — *I bought shoes **so that** I could wear them to the party*
Although – to suggest a contrast — ***Although** I don't have much money, I bought new shoes for the party*
However – to introduce a conflicting point — *I don't have much money, **however**, I bought new shoes for the party*
Because – to state a reason — *I bought new shoes **because** I am going to a party*
Or – to offer an option — *I had to choose between a new dress **or** new shoes for the party*
(Neither) Nor – to add an additional negative point — *I didn't buy socks **nor** a new dress, just new shoes*

Application of Conjunctions

1. Complete the following sentences with an appropriate conjunction. In some situations, more than one conjunction is acceptable.

   1. Cars are fast and convenient _____ are more expensive than public transportation.
   2. It is better to carpool with colleagues _____ traffic is reduced.
   3. Trains and boats are a great way to transport goods, _____ they are very slow.
   4. Saving money for the future is a great idea, _____ it can be difficult to do.
   5. Some families have a car _____ a family sized vehicle like a mini van.
   6. _____ bikes are a great, healthy way to get around, they are not always practical.
   7. City parks are a great place to bike, rollerblade _____ walk.
   8. Many people become nervous driving behind big trucks _____ they can't see anything beyond the truck.
   9. People can choose to park on the street _____ in a parking lot.
   10. On some roads, neither bikers _____ rollerbladers are allowed for safety reasons.

Exam practice: Reading part 3

B

The following text is missing some important words. The missing words could be prepositions, articles, verbs, etc.

Winnipeg has been a centre for transportation ¹_____ distribution across North America for over a century. The city is one of ²_____ most cost-effective locations in North America for business operations ³_____ of its low costs of electricity, reasonable real estate prices, ⁴_____ competitive wage rates. Winnipeg is located ⁵_____ the geographic centre of North America with a variety of distribution capabilities by ⁶_____, rail, and road and short-distance connections to Asia ⁷_____ Europe via polar routes. The major east-west route crossing Winnipeg is ⁸_____ Trans-Canada Highway, which runs between Victoria (BC), through Winnipeg, and east to St. John's (NL). It is the world's ⁹_____ national highway with a length of 7,821 km (4,860 miles). Winnipeg is located ¹⁰_____ a one-hour drive of the US border.

Vocabulary: Types of transportation

C Brainstorm the different types of transportation available. Think of man-powered, fuel powered and alternatively powered examples. Also think of air, land, rail and sea examples as well.

Application of types of transportation

1. Looking at your list above, answer the following questions with a partner.

    1. Which is/are the cleanest for the environment? Why?
    2. Which is/are the fastest? Most convenient?
    3. Which is/are the cheapest? The most expensive?

    How do you travel to work?

    How often do you use the different kinds of transportation?

    What is your favourite kind of car? Why?

    If you could have any car in the world, what would it be? Describe it in detail.

Exam practice: Reading part 4

D Read the following text about Winnipeg and answer the multiple choice questions that follow

After Canada's Confederation in 1867, and the creation of the Canadian Pacific Railway, Winnipeg was envisioned as a conduit between eastern and western Canada, and as long as the railway was the chief mode of transportation in Canada, it was exactly that. It is the capital of Manitoba and more than half of that province's population lives in the greater Winnipeg area.

Most of Canada's western cities were founded in the late 1800's, mostly by English explorers. But Winnipeg's history is ancient compared to all Canadian cities, and the first European settlements there were French and not English. To understand its history, one must understand the significance of its geographical location. Winnipeg is situated at the junction (also known as the confluence) of two major rivers, the Red and the Assiniboine. As such, this was a major transportation route for First Nations People, and archeological records of their inhabitation of the area that is now Winnipeg go back to prehistoric times.

The name "Winnipeg" comes from the Cree language, and means "muddy waters." It is only fitting that the name comes from a source of one of the local first nations, as there is even evidence that these prehistoric people farmed along the banks of the Assiniboine River. Yet, these waterways were also used by many other of the First Nations people, including Anishinaabe, Assiniboine, Ojibway and Sioux.

There are still many Cree and other First Nations people found in Winnipeg, including Metis, and yet it has more recently been a destination for people from all over the world, especially Filipinos. This influx, is to the extent that Tagalog, the native language of the Philippines, is the second most common language spoken there after English.

Winnipeg's modern history and character, while ever-evolving, really goes back to the arrival of the French in the early 1700's. The battle between the English and French for control of North America was in part played out in Winnipeg. It has been the scene of many rebellions, complicated by the emergence of the Metis Nation, and their spiritual leader, Louis Riel, who led the Red River Rebellion in 1869-70. Other violent confrontations such as the Winnipeg General Strike of 1919 all contributed to the colourful history of a very proud and unique Canadian community.

D Choose the best answer based on the information from the text.

1. When were the plans for Winnipeg's future as a hub thought of?
a) After Confederation
b) After Confederation but before the railway was built
c) After the railway was built
d) Once Confederation was established and the railway was built.

2. Most of the people in Manitoba live
a) In Winnipeg
b) In and around Winnipeg
c) Outside of Winnipeg
d) Around Winnipeg

3. Who settled the Winnipeg area?
a) The French
b) The English
c) The Metis
d) The First Nations People

4. Which First Nations farmed the area?
a) Assiniboine, Ojibway, Sioux and Metis
b) Assiniboine, Ojibway, Sioux
c) Anishinaabe, Assiniboine, Ojibway and Sioux
d) Assiniboine, Ojibway, Sioux and Cree

5. After English, which language is spoken by most people?
a) Metis
b) Cree
c) First nation language
d) Tagalog

6. Who was Louis Riel?
a) A French General
b) An English General
c) The mayor of Winnipeg
d) The leader of the Metis

Exam practice: Speaking part 2

E

1. Describe in detail where the following are located. Go Back to Unit One, Part C, exercise 2 for help if needed.

   1) Tim Horton's
   2) Best Western
   3) The Library
   4) The Church
   5) Gift shop

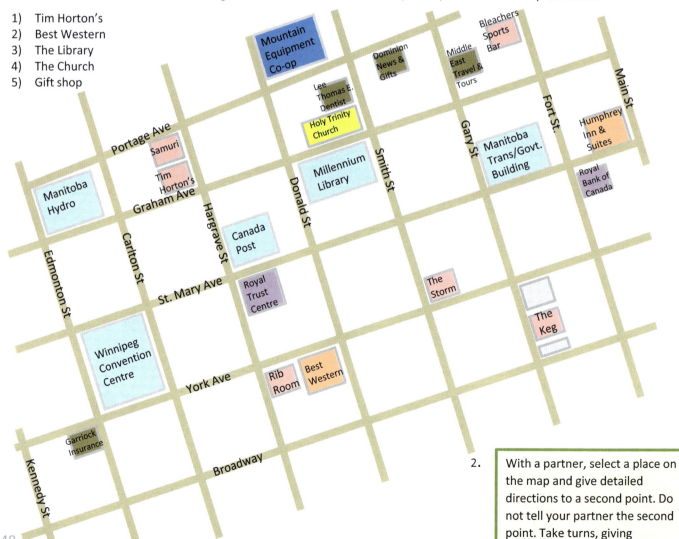

2. With a partner, select a place on the map and give detailed directions to a second point. Do not tell your partner the second point. Take turns, giving directions for 2 or 3 places.

Exam practice: Speaking part 3

F You are going to hear a news item about the current traffic conditions. Listen carefully and answer the following questions.

1. Would you say the report was mostly good news or bad news?
2. How many roads were the focus of the traffic report?
3. On which road were the emergency services located?
4. What advice was given to motorists?

Vocabulary: Money related vocabulary and collocations

G Write a word from the box into the correct sentences and definitions below.

Save up for	Invest/divest (in)	Income tax deductions	RRSP contributions	
Interest rates	Inheritance	Nest egg	Debit/credit	Devalue	Equity
Depreciate	Cash flow	Amortization period	Salary	Severance pay	

1. The _____ that she received when her mother passed away was spent on small meaningful things .
2. Every one that works is required to have _____ taken directly off their cheque.
3. When the factory closed down, everyone received a small _____.
4. Some people regularly _____ and _____ depending on the market.
5. It is good to buy a house when _____ are low.
6. As soon as you buy a car, it's value _____.
7. When starting a business, it is a good idea to make sure you have a strong _____.
8. It gives people a sense of pride when they finally _____ a big purchase .
9. It is never too late to start thinking about making _____ so you can have a comfortable retirement.
10. She saved a little bit of her paycheck every month so that she would have a nice _____ to add to her RRSP.
11. It is very difficult to live when your _____ is greater than your _____.
12. The _____ in Canada was recently reduced to 25 years from 30 to protect people from becoming 'house poor'.
13. When currency is _____ it refers to the official lowering in value against other currency.
14. Many people believe that earning a yearly _____ is better than being paid an hourly wage.
15. In order to receive a loan from most banks, you are required to have some kind of _____.

Review

Vocabulary to remember

Use this box to write any new vocabulary you learned in the unit

---

What advice would you give someone buying a house for the first time? Write a letter to a friend, giving them advice. Make sure to use vocabulary from this unit. Think about transportation as well. Will you advise them to buy close to the airport? Or maybe close to public transportation.

Describe a time where you made a large purchase. Maybe your first car, a house or another expensive item that you had to think about carefully. Write about the item, the circumstances and your feelings below.

How often do you go to the cinema?

Vocabulary: Art

A

What is art? How can we define art? Brainstorm the different kinds of art there are in the world.

oil paintings   movies   poetry

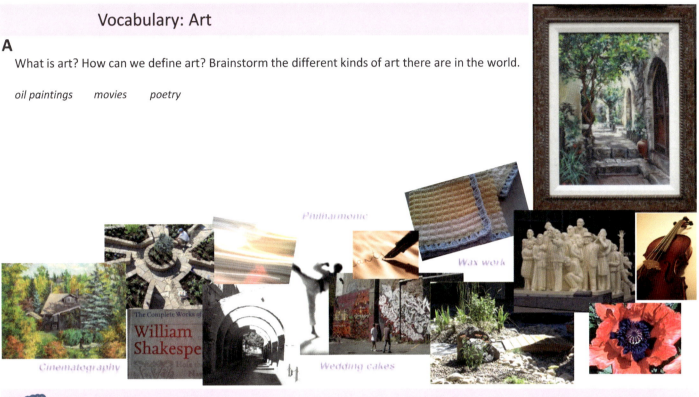

Talking about Art

1. What is your favourite kind of art? Think about it for a minute and make some notes. Why do you like it? What characteristics does it have that appeal to you?

Exam practice: Listening part 4

B You will hear short dialogues between 2 people. What is the purpose of the conversation? Look back at Unit Three, Part D, for review if needed.

1. The woman is
   a) suggesting
   b) making a complaint
   c) boasting
   d) expressing an opinion

2. The man is
   a) agreeing
   b) disagreeing
   c) persuading
   d) objecting

5. The man is
   a) stalling for time
   b) admiring the art
   c) thankful for a decision
   d) bargaining

6. The woman is
   a) making a request
   b) confirming
   c) reminding
   d) giving advice

3. The man is
   a) explaining
   b) showing pride
   c) expressing an opinion
   d) arguing

4. The woman is
   a) objecting
   b) explaining
   c) expressing relief
   d) demanding an apology

7. The woman is
   a) commanding
   b) insisting
   c) suggesting
   d) requesting

8. The man is
   a) expressing regret
   b) objecting
   c) arguing
   d) apologizing

Grammar: The passive

C

The passive construction is: **be + past participle**
We use the passive in academic writing, formal writing, business writing and when using higher levels of English. It is polite, non-accusative and is also important when we want to **focus on the object**.

Let's examine.
You saw your brother break a cup. You want to tell your mom. You will **not** use the passive because you want your brother to get into trouble! You would say…"Mooommmm! Johnny broke the cup" In this sentence, Johnny is the **subject,** the cup is the **object.** You don't want to be polite.

BUT!
You are waiting for an important email. You expected it 2 hours ago. In this situation, you would use the passive. You send an email to your co-worker, gently reminding them that you are still waiting. You ask politely….."Has that email been sent yet?" This is a much nicer way than saying…Have you sent it yet? Our focus is on the email, not the person who should have sent it.

In the above situation, we would use the present perfect and the passive. Notice how we change the form of 'be' to match our verb form.

To include 'the doer' of the action, add the word **by** followed by the person. *The Window was broken **by David**. The man was arrested earlier today **by police**.*

We also use the passive when we do not know 'the doer' of the action (*The window was broken last night)* or it is obvious (*The man was arrested earlier today)*. We don't know who broke the window. Only the police arrest people.

Application of The passive

1. Complete the following sentences with either the passive or active form. Make sure to use the correct tense as well.

    1. This beautiful piece of art _____ (paint) by a famous Russian-Canadian.
    2. The sculpture that _____ (recently, donated) to the gallery, is very valuable.
    3. The Juno awards _____ (hand out) every year to recognize Canadian musicians.
    4. She thoroughly enjoys _____ (take) pictures of old buildings.
    5. The book _____ (well write) however I didn't like how the movie _____ (make).
    6. She _____ (give) an award for her dedication to the gallery.
    7. I _____ (not bless) with artistic talents.

Exam practice: Reading part 4

D

Read the following text about Montreal and choose either *True* or *False*, for the multiple choice questions that follow

There is much to see in Montreal, as the city abounds in wonderful architecture that stretches back as far as the 1600's, which is very rare for a North American City. The city is in the process of restoring Old Montreal, where one can step back in time into the city as it appeared several centuries ago, complete with horse-drawn carriages and cobblestone streets.

Montreal is now Canada's second largest city (after Toronto). For many years, it has been considered Canada's cultural capital, as the city is absolutely vibrant with one the richest arts scene to be found anywhere in North America. Montreal is the home of many arts festivals, including music, film, theatre, dance, and even circus arts – it is the home of the world-famous Cirque de Soleil.

Summer in particular is when Montreal comes alive. The summer months are crammed with arts festivals, including fringe theatre, film, spoken word, dance, and all kinds of music as diverse as classical and Reggae and electronica, to name but a few. Perhaps the most famous of these is the Montreal Jazz Festival at the end of June, when the entire city becomes the stage for many of the world's greatest jazz musicians.

There are also festivals that celebrate many of the cultures that make up modern day Montreal, including Nuits d'Afrique (African Nights), Dragon Boat Racing, Montreal Highland Games, Italian Week, Matsuri Japan and of course, Canada Day on July 1st. There is an expression in French known as joi de vivre – which simply means the enjoyment or even delight in living. In Montreal, this is more than just a saying, it is a way of life, making Montreal unique among Canadian cities.

1. The buildings in Montreal are all old — True False
2. People only drive horses and carriages in Montreal — True False
3. Montreal is smaller than Toronto — True False
4. People know Montreal as the cultural capital of Canada — True False
5. Cirque du Soleil is from Montreal — True False
6. Many international jazz musicians travel to Montreal in June — True False

Exam practice: Reading part 3

E The following text is missing some important words. The missing words could be prepositions, articles, verbs, etc. Complete the text with an appropriate word.

One of ^{1} _____ earliest French explorers to visit North America was Jacques Cartier, who sailed up the St. Lawrence River ^{2} _____ 1535. At the base of ^{3} _____ small mountain he discovered a settlement of Iroquois people that ^{4} _____ been in existence for hundreds of years ^{5} _____ had over 1,000 inhabitants. This settlement was ^{6} _____ as Hoshelaga.

Incredibly, when a second French explorer, Samuel de Champlain, returned to the St. Lawrence River 70 years ^{7} _____, this community had vanished. Champlain established a fur trading fort at the ^{8} _____ location, which would centuries later become ^{9} _____ of Canada and the world's most vibrant cities – Montreal. For many years, Montreal remained as a trading post for the fur trading industry that ^{10} _____ critical to the economy of Canada prior to and at the time it ^{11} _____ declared a country in 1867. It ^{12} _____ incorporated as a city in 1832, and became the original capital of what was then referred ^{13} _____ as the Province of Canada (when Canada was a British colony). In 1849, the Parliament was burned to the ground during a protest and the Canadian capital was ^{14} _____ to Ottawa which was thought to be a safer location.

Pronunciation Tips

F

The following verb endings are commonly mispronounced or even dropped by students. If a word is not finished or if it is pronounced incorrectly, it makes it hard for the listener to follow the conversation easily.

Third person singular, possessive, plurals and contracted form: **s, es, ies, 's,**

Practice saying the following words, making sure you clearly pronounce the final **s** sound

makes   does   churches   dogs   washes   parties   she's

Regular past tense verbs

Words that end in **ted** or **ded**: pronounce an extra syllable →   wan•ted deci•ded
Words that end in **c, ch, ck, gh, k, p, pp, s, sh, ss, x**: the final sound is '**t**' no extra syllable →   wished   laughed
All other endings have a final sound of '**d**' →   canned   carved

1. How would you pronounce the following words? These are just some of the words that are frequently mispronounced.

walked	turned	likes	drives	students	glasses	cities
it's	studied	watched	goes	exams	colleagues	asked
Parked	finished	tried	tired	sewed	friends	knives
shoes	hers	whispered				

2. Can you think of other words that cause pronunciation difficulties? What words do you struggle with? Write them below and practice saying them correctly with the help of your teacher.

   Exam practice: Speaking part 2

G

Describe in detail what you see in the pictures below. Work with a partner and help each other to expand your answers.

Review

Vocabulary to remember

Use this box to write any new vocabulary you learned in the unit

Write a letter to a friend about a piece of art you have or would like to have. Describe it's appearance, the artist, why you like it and how you found it. Include both the active and passive construction.

Can you play an instrument? Are you a painter or can you draw? Think about your creative skills and describe them below. If you are not creative, describe a time you tried to create something and what was wrong with it.

What do you do?

Vocabulary: Work collocations and professions

A

We have many collocations in the world of work. Look at the following group of words and with a partner, discuss what they mean.

steady job	repetitive strain	meet standards
job security	incentive scheme	white collar
blue collar	made redundant	sick leave
in charge of	job performance	take over
industry specific	assembly line	work overtime
growing sector	demand for	un/skilled labourers

Application of Work collocations and professions

1. Complete the following sentences using words from the box above.

    1. It is important to have a _____ when deciding to buy a house.
    2. The _____ more competition in telecommunications has increased over the last 15 years.
    3. Those who work on an _____ often work fewer hours during economic slowdowns when people buy less.
    4. Big companies often _____ smaller neighbourhood stores as they expand.
    5. _____ workers are more likely to get greater benefits than _____ workers.
    6. Doing the same task over and over can lead to _____ injuries.
    7. Labour unions sometimes strike to gain _____.
    8. People are regularly promoted based on their outstanding _____.
    9. Managers are _____ other employees and the operations of a particular department.
    10. Employees who are seasonal workers are often _____ during other times of the year.

2. For the remaining new vocabulary, create a sentence showing your understanding of the words.

    1. Industry specific

    2. Growing sector

    3. Incentive scheme

    4. Meet standards

    5. Sick leave

    6. Un/skilled labourers

    7. Work overtime

B Now lets think of different kinds of jobs and professions. Write them below

C With a partner, discuss the following questions. Share your answers with the class

1. What do you think is the best job?
2. What do you think is the worst job?
3. What is your dream job?
4. What jobs have you done?
5. What is the most valuable job in society?
6. What are the most important aspects of a job?
7. How would you describe work in your country?
8. Does having a good work ethic really matter?

Exam practice: Reading part 3

D The following text is missing words. Complete the paragraph with an appropriate word. Then discuss your opinion in response to the text. Work with a partner to identify the missing words. This text is difficult and will provide you with many new words.

It [1] _____ be very difficult coming to a new country and becoming [2] _____ in a career. Success can depend [3] _____ many factors but ultimately your ability [4] _____ adapt to a new cultural environment and the unique perspectives therein will determine [5] _____ progress. Being able to maintain an [6] _____ mind and refrain [7] _____ categorically judging your new home will assist you [8] _____ achieving your goals. This does not by any means imply or [9] _____ conforming but rather integrating your own defined dogma and perspectives into a new atmosphere. Take cultural cues from your peers. Submerge [10] _____ into the day to day activities that are common in your area and don't be [11] _____ to ask questions.

1. Do you agree with the text? Can you think of any additional advice you would give to people moving to Canada? What about advice for people trying to get a job in your profession? Take a minute to think about it and make some notes below, then share with the class.

Exam practice: Listening part 5

E Listen to the following interview and answer the accompanying questions

1. What sector does she work in?

2. Which group of doctors is she talking about?
   a) Doctors in other countries
   b) Doctors from other countries
   c) Doctors going to other countries
   d) Doctors practicing medicine in other countries

3. How long has she been in her current job?
4. Why does she like it?
5. What skills does she suggest someone has entering this field?

6. Which 3 pieces of advice does she suggest
   a) respect, enjoyment, integrity
   b) Respect, culture, acting,
   c) Unconditional, people,
   d) enjoyment, range, ability, integrity

7. What kinds of integrity does she mention?

Introduction to Formal writing

In Part 2 of the writing exam, you are required to write a formal letter. In formal writing, the level of vocabulary is higher and we refrain from using colloquialisms or everyday language. They are fine to use in every day conversations, but try to use more formal vocabulary when writing formal letters. You will be marked on not only your vocabulary, but your grammar and your ability to organize your ideas. It is always extremely important to plan before you write, regardless of your writing skill level.

Books that contain synonyms and antonyms can often assist in formal writing. Be careful however. Sometimes several words are listed s synonyms but are context specific and will not suit your sentence. Some words to stay away from when writing formally include some of the following.
- because   Can you think of others?
- get
- things
- about

F In the following letter, some colloquial language has been used. Read through the letter and replace the informal words and phrases with more suitable words, found in the box on the following page. There may be more than one word or phrase per sentence.

Dear Hiring Manager,

I am writing this letter about the full time management job that was posted on the ABC job search website and to say that I have lots of experience . The opportunity shown in this listing is very nice, and I think that my experience and schooling make me the best person for this job.

There are several things that I can offer. I enjoy hard tasks, I can change to any situation as needed and enjoy helping my co-workers. I also have other good qualities, such as good customer service, I always want to be the best and have good communication skills. I also want to tell you that I am energetic, confident, and personable.

I hope that you will find my experience and interests match what you are looking for. I am sure that if I get this job, I will add value to you and your customers as a member of your team.

I can be reached anytime via my cell phone, 555-555-5555. Thank you for your time and consideration. I look forward to speaking with you about this employment opportunity. Please let me know if you have any questions.

Sincerely,
Jane Smith

regarding	adapt	believe	challenging	job (x3)	skills	inform
strong (x2)	obtain	express	assisting	strive for excellence		colleagues
appealing	suit	candidate	education	plenty of	notify	confident

Exam practice: Reading Part 2

G Examine the following chart and answer the accompanying questions

	Number employed in thousands		
	Both sexes	Men	Women
All industries	**17507.7**	**9187.7**	**8320.0**
Goods-producing sector	3872.0	3023.9	848.1
Agriculture	309.2	214.7	94.4
Forestry, fishing, mining, quarrying, oil and gas	369.1	298.7	70.4
Utilities	140.7	106.3	34.5
Construction	1267.5	1117.4	150.1
Manufacturing	1785.5	1286.8	498.7
Services-producing sector	13635.7	6163.8	7472.0
Trade	2643.8	1364.3	1279.5
Transportation and warehousing	849.4	647.9	201.4
Finance, insurance, real estate and leasing	1093.2	469.2	623.9
Professional, scientific and technical services	1299.3	750.5	548.8
Business, building and other support services	690.5	385.9	304.5
Educational services	1287.7	438.6	849.0
Health care and social assistance	2128.0	376.5	1751.6
Information, culture and recreation	790.4	438.2	352.2
Accommodation and food services	1102.4	453.7	648.7
Other services	795.3	358.5	436.8
Public administration	955.9	480.3	475.5

Source: Statistics Canada, CANSIM, table 282-0008 Last Modified: 2013-01-04.

1. Which sector employs the most people?

2. In that sector, which employs the most men?

3. Which industry employs the least women?

4. How many people in total are employed in the Educational Services Industry?

5. How many industries employ more women than men?

6. Which industry employs the most people?

💭 Do you think the numbers would be the same for your country? Think about the similarities and differences and discuss with the class.

Exam practice: Writing part 2

H Using the vocabulary from this unit and the various grammar we have learn throughout this book, create a cover letter for yourself. You can choose a real job from a job search website and practice what you should write. Your formal letter should be 150-175 words. Use the space below to make notes before you begin writing. Type your letter and print it. How long did it take? Keep practicing your typing skill so that you reduce your errors for the exam.

Review

Vocabulary to remember

Use this box to write any new vocabulary you learned in the unit

With a partner and using the job posting you found and the cover letter you wrote, take turns practicing interviews. You will be presenting your interview to the class for feedback and suggestions. Use the space below to make notes and create your interview.

Make a list of things to remember when you have a real interview. After your interview, your other classmates may have had some great suggestions or maybe you heard something from another interview you want to remember.

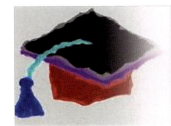

Are you ready?

Quiz about Canada

A What do you know about Canada? Take this quiz below to find out!

1. Is military service compulsory in Canada?
2. Which is the only official bilingual province in Canada?
3. Who was the first European to explore the St. Lawrence River?
4. What happened to Louis Riel?
5. Why do Canadians wear the red poppy on November 11th?
6. Who are the RCMP and what is their role?
7. How many provinces and territories does Canada have?
8. What is the capital of Canada?
9. How many people live in Canada?
10. How big is Canada?
11. Which city was the first to host the Winter Olympic Games in Canada? What year?
12. What is the name of Canada's most northern community?

Reading about Canada

B

1. Read the following passage and answer the questions to follow.

> If you look at a map of Canada, you will see that the majority of Canadians – about 75% -- live within 160 km (100 miles) of the United States border. Because most of us live in cities so far south, many Canadians have no idea what life is like further north. But again, looking at a map plainly shows that the greatest part of the country lies to the north.
>
> Travelling north, one finds that the trees and vegetation most of us are familiar with soon give away to the boreal forest, and then to tundra, and finally to the barren landscape of the high arctic. Obviously, there are not a lot of people inhabiting Canada's frigid north. Communities here are few and far between. The harsh climate and the vast distances involved mean that the only way settlements can be reached is by airplane.

1. Geographically, most of Canada exists within 160 kilometres of the US	True	False
2. Canadians don't travel north	True	False
3. The greatest people live in the north	True	False
4. The landscape is more barren in the north	True	False
5. There are many communities in the north	True	False
6. The people in the north always travel by plane	True	False

Speaking & reading about Canada

2.

Name	Date: From	Date: To	Political Party	Home City
Stephen Harper	2006	Present	Conservative	Toronto, Ontario
Paul Martin	2003	2006	Liberal	Windsor, Ontario
Jean Chretien	1993	2003	Liberal	Shawinigan, Quebec
Kim Campbell	1993	1993	Conservative	Port Alberni, British Columbia
Brian Mulroney	1984	1993	Conservative	Baie-Comeau, Quebec
John Turner	1984	1984	Liberal	(Richmond) – Rossland, British Columbia
Pierre Trudeau	1980	1984	Liberal	Montreal, Quebec
Joe Clark	1979	1980	Conservative	High River, Alberta
Pierre Trudeau	1968	1979	Liberal	Montreal, Quebec
Lester (Mike) Pearson	1963	1968	Liberal	Newtonbrook, Ontario
John Diefenbaker	1957	1963	Conservative	Neustadt, Ontario
Louis St Laurent	1948	1957	Liberal	Compton, Quebec
William Lyon Mackenzie King	1935	1948	Liberal	Berlin, Ontario
Richard B. Bennett	1930	1935	Conservative	Hopewell Cape, New Brunswick
William Lyon Mackenzie King	1926	1930	Liberal	Berlin, Ontario
Arthur Meighen	1926	1926	Conservative	Anderson, Ontario
William Lyon Mackenzie King	1921	1926	Liberal	Berlin, Ontario
Arthur Meighen	1920	1921	Conservative	Anderson, Ontario
Sir Robert Borden	1911	1920	Conservative	Grand Pre, Nova Scotia
Sir Wilfred Laurier	1896	1911	Liberal	Saint-Lin, Canada East
Sir Charles Tupper	1896	1896	Conservative	Amherst, Nova Scotia
Sir Mackenzie Bowell	1894	1896	Conservative	(Rickinghall) – Belleville, Ontario
Sir John Thompson	1892	1894	Conservative	Halifax, Nova Scotia
Sir John Abbott	1891	1892	Conservative	St. Andrews, Lower Canada
Sir John A Macdonald	1878	1891	Conservative	(Glasgow)– Kingston, Upper Canada
Alexander Mackenzie	1873	1878	Liberal	(Logierait) – York East
Sir John A Macdonald	1867	1873	Conservative	(Glasgow)– Kingston, Upper Canada

C With a partner, compare and contrast and summarize the information in the table above about the Prime Ministers of Canada. For example: *There have been 15 Conservative and 12 Liberal Prime Ministers of Canada. All but 5 former Prime Ministers were born in Canada.*

Now answer these questions.

1. Who was the longest serving Prime Minister?
   a) Sir John A. Macdonald   b) Sir Wilfred Laurier   c) Kim Campbell   d) William Lyon Mackenzie King
2. How many Prime Ministers were born in Ontario?
   a) 11   b) 9   c) 12   d) 10
3. Who is the only French-Canadian Conservative to be Prime Minister?
   a) Pierre Trudeau   b) Jean Chretien   c) Louis St Laurent   d) Brian Mulroney
4. How many Prime Ministers served less than a year?
   a) 4   b) 5   c) 6   d) 7

Writing to a friend about Canada

C Write a letter (125 words) to a friend or family member back home, telling them about your life in Canada. In your letter, you should include
  i. Where you live, describe the city, where it is and what there is to do
  ii. What the economy is like and the job situation (is it easy to get a job)
  iii. Talk about your family or friends that are here with you and how they like the city you are in.
  iv. When you plan on going home for a visit, invite them to Canada for a visit.

 ## Listening to the Canadian Anthem

D
1. Respond to what you have just heard.

    1. What is the tone ?

    2. How does it make you feel?

    3. What is your favourite part?

    4. Do you think it is a suitable anthem for Canada?

Speaking about Canada

E
1. There has recently been some controversy around the line '...*in all thy sons command!*' because it is not gender neutral. The original version was *'thou dost in us command'* but was changed to show support for soldiers away at war. Do you think it should be changed back?

    Think about your national anthem. Does it refer to men or women or is it gender neutral? What are your thoughts on changing national anthems to be more gender neutral?

2. Can you label the map of Canada below? Do you know the symbols and or flowers for each province and territory? What about the lakes and rivers? Oceans and seas? Capital cities? Use the space below the map to make some notes if you wish.

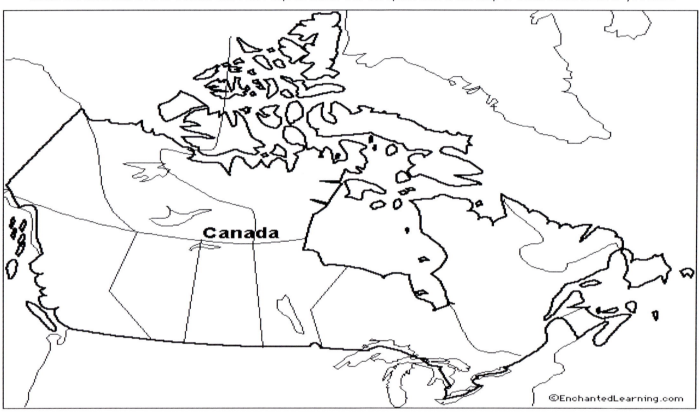

3. Can you think of any questions you have about Canada? They can be about anything and everything you want to know.

Appendix

Prepositions and common prepositional phrases

In a fight
In a blunder
In a bind
In a hurry
In a jiffy
In a matter of speaking
In a while
In due time
In over your head
In limbo
In mourning
In shock
In rehab
In talks with
In love
In a relationship
In hot water
In fear of

From a friend
From your perspective
From now on
From a reputable source
From nothing
From the start
From here on in

With that in mind
With a flare
With a friend
With regret
With help
With an iron fist

Up the creek
Up to no good
Up for something
Up in arms
Up and down

Down for the count
Down for it
Down and out
Down on your luck
Down with something

To say the least
To the west
To begin with
To school
To top it all off

Below the limit
Below the belt
Below the line

At last
At a crossroads
At your wits end
At your limit
At a point in life
At odds with
At a glance

Overjoyed
Over indulge
Overwrought
Overweight
Over extended
Over the moon
Over the hill
Over the shock

By the time
By all accounts
By way of

Before it starts
Before the storm
Before the calm
Before long
Before you know it

Without a doubt
Without a clue
Without reason
Without hope
Without you
Without experience
Without a chance
Without proof

Against all odds
Against the grain
Against time
Against the norm
Against your wishes
Against your better judgement

After all is said and done
After the dust settles
After the storm passes

For instance
For one thing
For your sake
For the millionth time
For eternity
For fun

On the edge
On the verge
On the run
On pogy
On the hook
On your nerves
On your last leg
On the other hand
On the flip side
On the contrary
On your mind

Under paid
Under staffed
Under weight
Under the bridge
Under the gun
Under your thumb
Under the impression
Under the weather

Above and beyond
Above all else
Above board
Above the line

In this book, we have not covered prepositions of time directly, however we have used them. Time phrases typically go at the end of a sentence but can also be found at the beginning and sometimes even in the middle.

In the morning
In the afternoon
In the evening
In a day
In a year
In June
In a moment
In 5 minutes
In 2013

We use **in** when we are talking about specific periods of time in which something will happen and a general idea within a defined 'block' of time. For example, we are specific when saying in June, however there are many days in June.

At noon
At the beginning
At the end
At 4pm
At dinner

We use **at** when we are talking about very specific periods of time when something will happen. There is nothing general about using this preposition of time.

On time	Something happens exactly when it is expected or supposed to happen
At the beginning	A fixed point when something started
In the beginning	A general guideline of time when something started
At the end	A fixed point when something ended
In the end	A general guideline of time when something started
Around 9am	An approximate time; could be before, could be after
Between 11-2	A range of time in which to expect something
Beyond 1984	Starting at the very end of something and continuing from that point onward
After school	A general idea of time to start at some point when something is completed
Before tomorrow	A general idea of time to start at some point from now to the time given

Phrasal verbs often give students a challenge as they are difficult to translate. While phrasal verbs are used in every day English, try to avoid using them in formal or business writing. Below are some common phrasal verbs and their meaning(s). Some phrasal verbs have more than one meaning so you must be mindful of the context.

Add up – make sense. *I don't understand. Your story doesn't add up. Am I missing something?*
Add up to – equal. *Five and 10 add up to 15.*
Ask around – inquire. *It is easier to ask around for the best restaurants than try them all.*
Bring up – raise, introduce for discussion. *The brought up 3 children. Please don't bring up the topic of my divorce.*
Break up – no longer together. *My friend and her boyfriend broke up the other day.*
Break down – stop working, non-functional. *My car broke down on the way. She had an emotional breakdown after his death.*
Break in – enter without permission, use until comfortable. *The thief broke into the store. She had to break in her new shoes.*
Break out – escape, come to the surface. *The prisoner broke out of jail. If you touch that plant, you will break out in a rash.*
Cut off – end. *His parents cut off his allowance.*
Cut in – interrupt. *She has a bad habit of cutting in on people during conversations.*
Cut down on – reduce. *The doctor said I should cut down on junk food*
Call off – cancel. *The baseball game was called off due to rain.*
Chip in – contribute. *Do you want to chip in for the wedding gift?*
Carry on – continue. *They carried on along the trail despite being lost.*
Drop out of – quit. *She wasn't interested in being a lawyer, so she dropped out of law school.*
Drop by – come/go to see someone. *His parents dropped by for a visit.*
Dress up – wear nice clothes. *She decided to dress up for her dinner date.*
Ease up – reduce pressure. *The driving instructor told the student to ease up on the gas pedal.*
End up – result. *We drove for hours and finally ended up in the next province.*
Figure out – solve. *The detectives had to figure out who the criminal was.*
Fall through – not to happen. *Our plans fell through and we stayed home.*
Find out – discover. *They were waiting to find out the results of the exam.*

Give up – surrender, quit. *After hours of trying to find her keys, she gave up. He gave up smoking 2 years ago.*
Get over – recover. *It took hi ages to get over his cold.*
Hand in – submit. *All employees had to hand in their time cards at the end of their shift.*
Jot down – make quick notes. *As he passed the store on the bus, he jotted down the number to call when he got home.*
Keep up – continue. *His boss told him to keep up the good work.*
Look into – investigate. *The police are looking into the recent crime in the area.*
Long for – yearn. *She longed for summer to return every fall.*
Leave out – omit. *By mistake, he left out important information on his application.*
Make do – manage. *She and her husband didn't have much money but they made do with what they had.*
Mix up – confuse. *She mixed up 2 numbers in the address and became lost.*
Point out – indicate/show. *The lecturer pointed out the mistakes in the student's argument.*
Pull out of – remove from participation. *After 3 hours, the runner pulled out of the race.*
Put forth – give. *The couple put forth an offer on the house.*
Run into – see unplanned. *I ran into an old friend from high school when I was on vacation.*
Show up – arrive. *It is considered rude to show up late to a dinner party.*
Show off – brag. *She likes to show off her money buy only wearing designer clothes.*
Sort out – organize/fix. *The employee had to sort out several issues before going home for the day.*
Take off – depart. *My plane takes off at 7pm, so I have lots of time.*

Common prefixes and suffixes. These are generally Latin in origin and have a fixed meaning on their own. They can sometimes change the perspective of a word. Recognizing these will help with some new vocabulary and identifying the word form being used.

Prefixes	Examples
Pre – before	premature
Post – after	post-graduate
Dis – negative implication	discourage
Non – without or lacking	non-verbal
Pro – in favour of	pro-health
Anti – against	anti-war
Over – too much	overpaid
Under – not enough	undercooked
Trans – across a framework/network or distance	transportation
Inter – including more than one component, person or thing	internet
Uni – one, solo	uniform
Bi – two	bicycle
Tri – three	trimester
Micro – small focus	microwave
Macro – large focus	macrobiotic
Semi – half	semidetached
Auto – manual, without instruction	automatic
Sub – below	submarine
Mono – consisting of one	monotone
Co – together	cohabitate
Circum – around	circumnavigate

Noun suffixes

-sion: discussion
-ation: imagination
-ness: goodness
-less: homeless
-hood: neighbourhood
-ment: encouragement
-cian: musician
-ship: friendship
-ence: existence
-ity: possibility

Adjective endings

-al: personal
-ial: financial
-ful: beautiful
-ous: nervous
-ly: friendly

Common Synonyms

Big – huge, gigantic, enormous, broad, large
Happy – delighted, cheery, content, pleased
People – individuals, folk, citizens, the public
Hard – difficult, challenging, complicated, tiring
Use – employ, utilize, operate, apply
Job – task, position, responsibility, appointment
Stop – cease, finish, terminate, halt

Small – tiny, miniscule, mini, compact
Sad – upset, down, gloomy, blue
Animals – creatures, wildlife, pets, living thing
Easy – simple, plain, effortless, a cinch
Help – aid, assist, do a favour, lend a hand
Start – begin, commence, create, launch

Common Antonyms

Big – small	Happy – sad	Hard – easy	Help – hinder	Start – Stop	Begin – end	Like – dislike
Love – hate	Warm – cool	Hot – cold	Wet – dry	Smooth – rough	Exciting - boring	

Common homonyms

Two	too	two
They're	there	their
Flower	flour	
Whole	hole	
Break	brake	
Aisle	I'll	isle
Ate	eight	
Bare	bear	
Blue	blew	
Close	clothes	
Cereal	serial	
Chilly	Chile	chili
Site	sight	cite

Modal verbs

can – could	will – would	shall – should	must – had to
may	might	ought to	

Modal verbs refer to possibility, ability and capability. They can be used when giving opinions, making suggestions, communicating your intentions.

After modal verbs, always use the infinitive form of your main verb, regardless of time and construction. For example, *She might go to school, she might have gone to school, she might have been tempted to go to school, she ought to have been going to school, she had to have been too busy to go to school.*

Common verb + preposition combinations

Interested in	aware of	depends on	different from	agree with	pay for	abide by
Belong to	think about	according to	affected by	experienced in	divide into	unaware of
Terrible at	wait for	jealous of	participate in	similar to	disagree with	based on
Because of	ashamed of	eligible for	impose on	illustrated by	laugh at	recover from

Use the following answers to make questions. The first one is done for you.

1. At the post office_____Where can I buy stamps_____?
2. 16 or 17_____?
3. Almost everyday_____?
4. My grandmother_____?
5. In my pocket _____?
6. Very hot_____?
7. By train_____?
8. About 20 minutes_____?
9. Because I am tired _____?
10. At the bookstore _____?
11. More than $500_____?
12. In June _____?
13. To the store_____ _____?
14. A book _____?
15. Only in Canada_____?

16. Football_____?
17. Salt and pepper_____?
18. Friendly_____?
19. Very good_____?
20. Maybe 3 kilometers_____?

Put the verbs in brackets into present simple, present perfect **or** past simple

1. John_____(go) to Warsaw last Tuesday.
2. I_____(never be) to the mountains.
3. We _____(be) here for three years now.
4. The Fishers usually _____(spend) their weekends in the country.
5. My father_____(be) born in Switzerland.
6. I_____(not hear) from John since he _____(go) to China in 2003.
7. We_____(have) to sell our grandparents' house last year.
8. Chris_____(leave) Spain three years ago and he_____(be) abroad since then.
9. Here you_____(be), finally! We have been waiting for you!

Put the verbs in brackets into present simple/continuous, present perfect simple/continuous **or** past simple/continuous

10. I _____(stay) here until next Friday.
11. My parents _____(stay) in Rome for three weeks now.
12. We usually _____(have) bread and butter for breakfast, but today we_____(have) fried eggs.
13. I _____(stay) this hotel since Friday.
14. Peter is not here yet. I _____(think) he has missed the train.
15. Because it is snowing, I _____(take) a taxi.
16. I still _____(not find) the cd I _____(buy) last week.
17. I _____(try) to solve this problem for the last two hours.
18. Call an ambulance! There _____(just be) an accident.
19. He_____(solve) these problems for three hours, but he_____(not solve) any yet.

Put the verbs in brackets into present simple/continuous, present perfect simple/continuous past simple/continuous **or** past perfect simple/continuous

20. I _____(live) in London many years ago.
21. I_____(live) in London and I work there.
22. I_____(live) in London at the moment, but will leave soon.
23. I_____(live) in London when Kennedy was assassinated.
24. I_____(live) in London for a few years when that happened.
25. Where _____(you put) the key? I cannot find it anywhere!

Adjective	Comparative	Superlative

Word families: When introduced to a new word, identify the other forms. Some are easy to identify (*inform, information, informative*) while others are not (*steal, theft, thieving*). Some so not have all forms

Verb	Noun	Adjective	Adverb	-/opposite	Other

| Verb | Noun | Adjective | Adverb | -/opposite | Other |

Be	Begin	Can	Speak
Buy	Hit	Give	See
Let	Forget	Eat	Teach
Write	Take	Know	Stand
Do	Feel	Lend	Catch
Ride	Spill	Lay	Hide

spoke spoken	could been able	began begun	was/were been
saw seen	gave given	hit hit	bought Bought
taught taught	ate eaten	forgot forgotten	let let
stood stood	knew known	took taken	wrote written
caught caught	lent lent	felt felt	did done
hid hidden	laid laid	spilled/t spilled/t	rode ridden

Leave	Run	Go	Become
Beat	Hang	Choose	Swim
Tear	Shine	Bite	Break
Rise	Sink	Meet	Steal
Throw	Wake	Dig	Feed
Come	Sleep	Hear	Drink

became become	went gone	ran run	left left
swam swum	chose chosen	hung hung	beat beaten
broke broken	bit bitten	shone shone	tore torn
stole stolen	met met	sank sunk	rose risen
fed fed	dug dug	woke woken	threw thrown
drank drunk	heard heard	slept slept	came come

Make	Think	Say	Drive
Tell	Shut	Fall	Cost
Must	Send	Cut	Learn
Pay	Get	Wear	Have
Read	Sit	Smell	Spend
Put	Understand	Sell	Set

drove driven	said said	thought thought	made made
cost cost	fell fallen	shut shut	told told
learned/t learned/t	cut cut	sent sent	had to had to
had had	wore worn	got got	paid paid
spent spent	smelled/t smelled/t	sat sat	read read
set set	sold sold	understood understood	put put

Bend	Ring	Win	Shake
Burn	Light	Lie	Show
Blow	Draw	Fight	Hear
Hurt	Kneel	Forgive	Fly
Hold	Sing	Mean	Lose
Build	Bring	Find	Freeze

shook shaken	won won	rang rung	bent bent
showed shown	lay lain	lit lit	burned/t burned/t
heard heard	fought fought	drew drawn	blew blown
flew flown	forgave forgiven	knelt knelt	hurt hurt
lost lost	meant meant	sang sung	held held
froze frozen	found found	brought brought	built built

Keep	Dream	Grow	Burst
Lead	Spoil	Stick	

Cut out these irregular verbs to make cue cards for convenient study on the go!

burst burst	grew grown	dreamt/ed dreamt/ed	kept kept
	stuck stuck	spoilt/ed spoilt/ed	led led

		come	blow		
	slept				drawn
		heard		fought	
	drank				hurt
make				knelt	
think			forgive		
		said	fly		
	drove			held	
tell					sung
		shut		meant	
	fell		lose		
cost					built
		had to		brought	
	sent		find		
cut				froze	
learn			keep		
	paid				dreamt
		got		grew	
	wore		burst		
have				led	
		read	spoil		
	sat				stuck
smell				spent	
		bent	put		
	rang				understood
		won		sold	
	shook		set		
burn					been
light				began	
		lain			Been able
	showed			spoke	

leave		
buy		
		hit
	gave	
see		
		run
	let	
forget		
		eaten
	taught	
go		
write		
	took	
		known
	stood	
become		
		done
	felt	
		lent
	caught	
		beaten
	rode	
spill		
lay		
		hidden
	hung	
swim		
		torn
	shone	
bite		
		chosen

	broke	
rise		
sink		
	met	
		stolen
	threw	
wake		
		dug
	fed	

Photocopy this irregular verb quiz to maximize your practice!

Use this page to make notes and to write down things you want to remember.

Acknowledgements

Every effort has been made to acknowledge the creators of clip art and stock photos. Many of the original websites and urls associated with the imaged used in this book have been changed or altered and while I have spent hours upon hours trying to locate and establish new links or reference, some images I simply cannot locate. If anyone recognizes clip art images as theirs, please let me know. If not mentioned, the composition or graphic, photo or information has been created by me, Christina Burnside. All explanations, activities, questions, format and content in this course book has been decided upon and developed by myself unless stated below.

I would like to thank my family and friends for their support during this project.

Unit One: Banner – dmstudio (Older version of image used not available); Airport sign – 123RF.com.
Unit Two: Banner – unavailable; Conversation circle – canstock (previous version used).
Unit Three – Banner – unavailable; Picture 1 – Raymond Ladd, Kevin Ladd, Travis Ladd, Christina Burnside; Picture 2 – Riley Paterson, Meredith Whipp, Kevin Paterson, Donna Paterson, Emily Paterson, Donald Taylor, Carolyn Taylor; Picture 3 – various family; Picture 4 – Lloyd Davis, Donald Taylor, unknown; Picture 5 – extension.org; Picture 6 – beerlodgefellas.com; Queen City of the Plains composition – Eugene Stickland; Activity F text – Eugene Stickland.
Unit Four: Banner – udoerasmus.com; Food guide charts – Health Canada; Pizza – fanpop.com; Grise Fiord composition – Eugene Stickland; picture of Grise Fiord – canadiangeographic.ca, Junk Food – neurobodyfit.com.
Unit Five: Banner – Dixie Allen (about.com); Picture 1 – City of Ottawa; Picture 2 – City of Ottawa; Picture 3 – Ottawa Life Magazine, Jennifer Chauhan; Picture 4 – City of Ottawa; Picture 5 (faded tulips behind reading) – City of Ottawa; Picture 6 – City of Ottawa.
Unit Six: Banner – Andrija Markovic; Group of 3 pictures – 1-bellacc.com, 2 – detox-heavymetals.com, 3 – George Hamilton, Vancouver Sun; Water pollution picture - http://blog.lib.umn.edu/schne644/architecture/2008/04/; park/marina/mountains picture – link no longer active.
Unit Seven: Train and skyline – northernontariobusiness.com; Truck – ecomonicdevelopmentwinnipeg.com; Riverview – relocationwinnipeg.com; Money in hands – Winnipeg Sun.
Unit Eight – Banner: tkshare.com; Collage (from left to right) – landscape painting -Larisa Nikonova, landscaping - Peter Taylor, abstract, black & white, Shakespeare photo - Christina Burnside, martial arts - 123rf.com, graffiti - assandrapages.com; calligraphy pen - http://curgol.blogspot.ca/2009/05/calligraphy-pens.html, crochet blanket - Christina Burnside, landscaping - Peter Taylor, city sculpture - 123rf.com; landscape painting - Larisa Nikonova, flower - Christina Burnside, Violin - picstopin.com; Larisa Nikonova; Montreal composition – Eugene Stickland x2; Vieux Montreal; loewshotels.com.
Unit Nine: Banner – gograph.com; dentist - Faculty of dentistry, dal.ca; ship yard - Nova Scotia Government photo; job fair - greaterhalifax.com; Dalhousie campus - dal.ca; construction workers – halifaxconstruction.ca.
Unit Ten: Canada reading – Eugene Stickland;

I would also like to thank the following people for their voices used in the recordings throughout this book: Eugene Stickland, Jeff Nelson, Laura Addington, Jyde Heaven, Sandra Taylor, Sarah Quirk, Amanda Quirk, Dave Sutherland, Kelly Woo